The Unity Oracle

A spiritual adventure to save the world

Joseph Drumheller

Joseph Drumheller
703 W. 7th, #320
Spokane, WA 99203 USA
www.josephdrumheller.com

© Copyright 2015, Joseph Drumheller. All rights reserved under International and Pan American Copyright Conventions. No part of this book may be reproduced, stored in a retrieval system, or transcribed, in any form or by any means — electronic, mechanical, photocopying, recording, or otherwise — without prior written permission from the publisher.

Cover Design: Joseph Drumheller

Cover Photo: Peter Bower

Sunburst Image: nikdoorg www.fotosearch.com

Editing: Julie Winter

ISBN-13:978-1511584609
ISBN-10:1511584602

Chapter 1
Animal Totems

Every day for the past three weeks, it had been the same. Never, for a split second, had he grown tired of it. Now that it was down to his last two days, his excitement was actually growing. He wanted to relish every second.

As the helicopter slowly descended from about 500 feet, J. C. Sananda, or Jason as he was affectionately called, was lowered onto the arctic tundra. It was a wilderness so enormous, it could have easily been described as an endless ocean of land. Jason was in heaven.

He was sent there in late August in the early 1990s as a geologist. They were searching for base metals in and around the Delong Mountain range of northern Alaska. To Jason, this untouched immensity was spectacular, even mystical. It touched his soul and exposed him to a spirit of the Earth he'd never known before. This was a living landscape; not only the wildlife and plant-life but the sky, the wind, the rivers, the colors, the sun, the light and the dark. *Everything* was alive. Jason could feel it to the core of his being. Furthermore, the particular place he was visiting this day, exuded more aliveness than any other. This was a place of power. This was Chevron Mountain.

Chevron Mountain was on the northern periphery of his field area. Forming the headwaters of the Wulik River, this spectacular pinnacle was formed from pushed up sedimentary rocks. The resulting eroded cliff faces were similar to the chevron stripes on an army sergeant's sleeve, hence the name, Chevron Mountain. In terms of mineral exploration, it wasn't considered a high priority. They were only going to give it a brief look on the last day of their expedition. However, for Jason, this area captured his interest like no other. He had a gut feeling; something about this mountain was special. He was sure something notable would stand out. A gnawing intuition pulled him in like an invisible magnetic force.

In fact, it was more than a gut feeling. Several times during the previous three weeks, Jason had several phenomenal encounters with wildlife along the creeks that flowed down from Chevron Mountain. Each encounter seemed more unusual than the previous. Jason had read numerous stories about animal totems and their mystical connections between native people, the Earth, and the Great Spirit. However, up until his recent experiences, Jason considered those stories powerful but strictly native folklore. They were something a white man best not mess around with. But now, with several captivating encounters in his back pocket, the possibility of a spiritual connection between him, the land, and the animals was centered smack-dab in the bull's eye of his personal radar.

Bubba
On the first full day of the expedition, Jason was without a work partner. Due to nasty weather in Fairbanks, his partner's flight was delayed, so he wasn't scheduled to arrive in camp until the next day. Jason's only option was to work alone. However, he'd never done that before, mainly because working companionless in the Alaskan bush was against safety protocol. But there was no way Jason was going to sit on his bum in camp all day. Plus, he rationalized, there would be a team of two other geologists working less than a mile away. It would be safe enough. So over breakfast, Jason successfully campaigned the entire crew into letting him go solo, just for the one day.

Apparently, with all his campaigning, Jason didn't get enough breakfast. All he could think about on the flight out to the field were brownies made by the camp cook Bea. She made them fresh from scratch that morning and they were still warm in his backpack. They weren't going to last for two seconds, once he got out on the ground and set his pack down.

On the flight in, the helicopter pilot noted a mammoth boar grizzly bear roaming for ground squirrels about two miles north of Jason's work area.

"Wow, take a look at that," he squawked through his headset. "Ol' fuzzy buns looks like he weighs in somewhere around 1200 pounds. He's huge."

They'd seen plenty of bears on this expedition and didn't expect any trouble from a bear two miles away. Nevertheless, Jason kept the bear's position in the back of his mind.

Jason was dropped off by the helicopter at the mouth of a small drainage flowing directly off Chevron Mountain. One glance to the east and Jason could see the prominence of the small but intriguing peak, several miles away. Once the chopper lifted off, he hiked about a quarter of a mile up the drainage, threw off his pack, and did something else he'd never done before. He started off his day by eating lunch.

As Jason began to aggressively ransack his backpack to find Bea's brownies, he heard a squelch on his walkie-talkie.

"Hey, is anybody working in the gulch to the east, below Chevron Mountain?"

It was fellow geologist, Dennis, a few hundred yards to the west. Jason knew Dennis was calling him, so he promptly ignored the call. He thought walkie-talkies were great tools but should never be put in the hands of someone like Dennis. He was on the bloody thing all day long just so he could hear himself talk. Dennis bugged the crap out of Jason when he was on a walkie-talkie.

About 10 seconds later, Dennis chimed in again.

"Hey, is anybody working in the gulch to the east, below Chevron Mountain? If so, there's a bear about a mile off to the north. No biggie, just a heads up."

They'd had plenty of encounters with bears by that time, without incident. It was no big surprise. So, once again, Jason made the note and placed the bear on his mental map. He squawked back to Dennis.

"Jason here. I'm in the gulch to the east. Thanks for the heads up on the bear. Got it."

As soon as he stuffed the radio back in this pack, he thought to himself, "Hmm...Fuzzy's wandered this way a bit. I'll give him a look in the binoculars in a couple of minutes." Then he returned to matters of a much higher importance, namely Bea's brownies.

About five minutes and three less brownies later, Dennis screamed down the hand held radio.

"Hey Jason. Incoming! Get the hell out of there now!"

Dennis was working with a another geologist by the name of Katy, a few hundred yards to the west of Jason. What they witnessed put Dennis into a state of semi-controlled hysterics and Katy on the trembling verge of tears. The bear got a whiff of Bea's delectables and made a 40 mile-an-hour sprint, straight for Jason. Apparently, the bear and Jason had at least one thing in common. They had a passion for fine homemade desserts.

As soon as Dennis sounded the echoing bear alarm, Jason dropped everything (including his cherished Bea's confections) and picked up his 12-gauge shotgun. The shotgun was loaded with one round of double ott buckshot, followed by four rounds of 7/8 ounce, 383 grain slugs. The massive amount of artillery ammo was designed for intimate encounters with 1200-pound fuzzy wuzzies.

Jason immediately scrambled up the 10-foot bank of loosely consolidated dirt and rocks. In a matter of seconds, he reached the flat tundra and turned to look over his shoulder. What he saw left an indelible image, permanently etched into the physical hardware of his brain. Thirty yards away, across a minuscule tundra drainage, was a bear. Only the word "bear" didn't quite fit the creature staring straight at him with a very aggressive I-know-no-predators attitude.

The instant Jason set eyes on the bear, he was immediately transported 230 million years into the past. He didn't see a bear. What he saw was a 14-foot tall, half-ton, furry, man-eating dinosaur, a massive carnivore that just bolted one mile in less than 90 seconds. The bear's immensity blew away any sense of Jason's proportioned reality. He simply had no reference for a living creature that big. He felt like he was hit by lightning and went straight into shock.

Somehow, Jason was able to keep an element of wit about him. He slowly turned and walked away. With his heart pounding about 200 beats per second, he kept saying to himself, "Don't run, don't run, don't run." From somewhere in the recesses of his subconscious mind, he remembered that running can entice a bear to charge. Not that that mattered. He knew he was dead meat. He'd never felt so naked. There's nowhere to go on the tundra, no superman phone booth to hop into. Plus, there was no way his little 5-shot pop gun would be worth a damn. He wasn't supposed to use it until a bear was within 10 yards. He was shaking so hard, he wouldn't have been able to hit water if he fell out of a boat, let alone a bear at 10 yards. His raging heart would certainly give out long before the bear got within range anyway. He knew he was a goner for sure, as he felt a warm liquid dribbling down his right leg.

Meanwhile, several hundred yards to the west, Dennis and Katy were able to watch the entire scenario unfold. Neither of them, in all there arctic exploration days, had ever seen an enormous animal move so fast. The bear covered a vast stretch of tundra in a matter of seconds. It was horrifying to watch with their colleague waiting innocently at the finish line. However, with all the cool, calm and collectedness of fumbling maniac, Dennis was somehow able pull a hand flare from his vest. Meanwhile, Katy was flirting with a nervous breakdown.

As he continued to tremble and shake, Dennis put on his readers and read the directions on the side of the flare. All the while, the bear was in a full gallop toward the pastry case.

"Okay…unscrew cap," Dennis mumbled.

Katy wailed, "Oh my God! Hurry!"

Trembling, he continued, "Extend arm with flare…Point toward sky…Pull chain."

POP…FIZZZZZZ…was the sound of the red flaming ball, as it lofted in an arch toward the bear. It landed about 10 yards away from the beast and he immediately lurched, turned, and ran in the opposite direction…for only about 20 feet. When the bear realized the red fireball on the ground wasn't going anywhere, he stopped and looked around. For the first time, he saw three two-legged critters on the horizon. Then, with a body language that said, "This is boring," he turned away and promptly went back to sniffing the tundra for ground squirrels.

Sweating profusely, Jason crossed the river (without touching the water) to join Dennis and Katy. Dennis had his .45 caliber pistol unholstered to add a little Indian Jones flair. It was an attempt to unsuccessfully impress Katy. Jason plopped on the river bank and continued to mumble and shake for the next several hours. He also fixed his gaze on the bear as it slowly disappeared over the horizon. Once the bear was gone, it took every ounce of courage Jason could muster to go across the river and retrieve his backpack. There was still one remaining brownie, from then on, lovingly referred to as Bear Bait.

Jason had other encounters with bears on the expedition but none as intense as that one. In fact, from that day on, he earned the nicknamed Bearman. One of the female geologist refused to work with him in the field after that.

She said, "He dangerous, all he does is attract bears."

And she was dead serious. However, Jason put a more humorous spin on it and that night wrote a song entitled, "I Got the Second on the Food Chain Blues."

Baby Bear
Several days later, Jason was working on a ridge that extended east from Chevron Mountain. It was a fascinating day out but not much in the way of turning up a mineral deposit. As the day wound down, a misty drizzle sprinkled from the sky. Tired, Jason donned his rain gear and kicked back into the tundra to take a quick mosquito infested nap. The arranged helicopter pickup time was still 30 minutes away. Soon after, he was awakened in mid-snore by the chopping blades of an approaching helicopter. The 4:30B was right on time. When Jason got the nod from the pilot, he threw his samples and gear into the rear hatch and climbed aboard.

Jason asked the pilot to fly up a north trending drainage that came off the south side of Chevron Mountain. He'd be working there the next day. Jason liked to get a bird's eye view of his working area the day before, just to make sure there were no surprises. As the chopper cruised up the drainage and took a modestly sharp corner, there was a mother grizzly and a single yearling cub. The pilot lifted up and took immediate evasive action. Helicopters are imposing beasts in the wild and they took every means to avoid harassing wildlife. However, as the chopper turned in the opposite direction, Jason saw the bears were severely agitated, running helter-skelter over the closest and steepest ridge. Watching the distress it caused the bears, Jason and the pilot felt pretty sheepish. Neither of them said anything on the rest of the flight back to camp.

The next day, Jason was slowly working his way up the steep drainage he'd flown over the day before. He knew the frightened bears were miles.

Exhausted by the strain of the climb, he sat down on a rock to take a breather and pulled out his water bottle for a drink. As he gulped water into his parched brisket, he saw something peculiar on a rock about five feet away.

It was the shape of a lima bean, only much bigger—about three inches long. It reminded Jason of Thanksgiving because it looked exactly like a fresh uncooked turkey gizzard. His analytical mind went into overdrive. "What the…? Where the heck did this come from? This is fresh meat…looks like it's only been here less than a day. Fresh meat doesn't last long around here. Some predator will pick this up before nightfall. Did this fall out of some other geologist's lunch? Couldn't be, nobody else is working within 100 miles from here. Is it a poorly digested wolf dropping? Nah… What the heck is it?" He couldn't figure it out, so he pulled out the magnifying glass that was dangling around his neck to take a closer look. What he saw sank a brick of guilt into the pit of his stomach.

As he ran his hand lens over the lima bean shaped meat, he could make out little features. There was a small white head and what looked like little paws. It appeared to be a tiny bear cub. Jason thought it was an aborted fetus from the grizzly bear sow the helicopter had spooked the day before. The chopper literally scared the life out of mama bear. This was a sad moment, indeed. However, Jason wasn't positive, so he put it in a small sandwich bag a took it back to camp. He wanted to show his colleagues and get their opinions.

Everyone agreed; it was a bear fetus. That certainly put a dent in camp morale. It also upped their awareness about the need to leave wildlife alone. Furthermore, Jason was becoming recognized by his fellow workers as something more than just a Bearman joke. Even these educated white folks suspected he may have a little bear medicine in him. So, following Jason's lead and with as much respect as the geology crew could muster, they reverently went down to the stream north of camp and buried the baby bear.

The Great White Wolves
A few days later, Jason was exploring further up the same drainage where he had the fated Bear Bait Brownie incident. He was plodding east, heading up an ankle-deep stream toward Chevron Mountain. As the stream shallowed and narrowed, it formed into a small canyon with spectacular sheer walls, about 10 to 20 feet high.

As he continued upstream, the canyon opened up into something like a circular arena, about 100 feet in diameter. Jason stepped into the opening and felt like a gladiator walking out into a miniature version of the Colosseum in Rome. Shading his eyes, he wandered into the center and marveled at the surrounding spectacle. He surveyed the canyon rim and spun around, 180-degrees, to take it all in. That's when he saw a flash of white out of the corner of his eye.

Jason spun around to focus in on the peripheral white flash. But whatever it was, was gone. It vanished instantaneously and in silence. However, what he saw in its place were two dead caribou. They didn't die from old age either. Both had open wounds in their necks and one was still slightly bleeding. Jason knew instantly that these were wolf kills and the flash of white he saw out of the corner of his eye was an Arctic Wolf. This was a rare sighting extraordinaire.

Jason was alarmed but not panicked. He still had his shotgun which could adequately dispatch any aggressive wolf. Furthermore, just as Jason expected, these wolves behaved like other wolves he'd seen. They scattered at the first hint of human presence. However, he didn't want to linger in case a grizzly was in the area. A grizzly around food is a much different story than a wolf.

Jason made haste continuing his trek, distancing himself from the scene of the crime. As he turned upstream, a shadow darted across the canyon floor. Glancing up he saw not one but three white wolves. They were looking down on him, as if nothing could be more natural. Their demeanor was neither frightened nor threatening. They seemed glad Jason was there, like they were proudly showing off their handiwork. Jason took it as an act of showmanship, honored to be the audience beholding their craft. Then, with a gentle bow of appreciation, Jason exited the canyon and continued marching upstream. It was the most spectacular animal encounter he'd ever had. Jason had come face to face with the spirit of the Wolf.

At the end of the day, he wanted to share his experience and show the wolf kill to his workmates. However, high winds and bad weather were moving in. There was no time to waste in flying back to camp. The wolf kill would have to wait. The storm continued into the next day, leaving the crew grounded at base camp.

When the weather cleared, Jason took two of his fellow colleagues to see the dead caribou. Not wanting to disturb the site, the helicopter dropped them off a few miles downstream. They hoofed it the rest of the way. When they arrived in the canyon opening, Jason couldn't believe his eyes. The wolves were long gone. All that was left of the caribou were pure white bones. In less than 48 hours, the wolves had completely cleaned both carcasses. There was absolutely nothing left. Jason had a difficult time convincing his colleagues the kill was only two days old.

From then on, Jason knew that stumbling on a wolf kill and actually seeing the wolves was far more than lucky. It was miraculous. And this…was only the beginning.

Chapter 2
Mineral Exploration

Copper meets Iron
Let's drift back to where our story began. It was Jason's second-to-last day in the arctic and he'd just been dropped off near Chevron Mountain. The recent memory of the bear and wolf encounters were on the forefront of his mind, as he began his slow trek east. He was excited to see what other surprises the mountain had in store. He was also mildly alarmed to discover he was a bit nervous. He felt the power of the mountain in the base of his gut, which stirred an uncomfortable and jittery reverence. Plus, he was working alone again. After three weeks in the bush, none of Jason's colleagues would step foot on the tundra with him, for fear of being eaten. He attracted animal encounters wherever he went. If Jason wanted to get eaten that was fine. But he wasn't going to take the rest of the crew down with him. To hell with safety protocol. So off he went, excited, cautious, nervous, respectful and alone.

Jason's approach up the mountain was from the west. He was dropped off about a mile upstream from the wolf kill arena. From there, he would work his way north, across a tundra expanse, then up to a ridge. At that point, he would turn east and follow the ridge up to a glacial bench, a hundred feet of or so beneath the summit. There was no need to climb to the top. From a geologic standpoint, he could see all he needed from the bench. Plus, the last hundred feet were steep and cliffy and there was no need to take a risky climb by himself. From the canyon stream to the glacial bench, the entire hike was about four or five mildly strenuous miles.

As soon as the helicopter left him behind, Jason felt a vast solitude he'd never felt before. It wasn't loneliness, it was much deeper and more profound. As he started his trek north, he became increasingly aware of the feeling. He felt like his entire body and energy field were opening up to connect with the tundra. With each step he took, the feeling expanded and deepened. After about a mile, he realized what it was. He was feeling the energy of the Earth. In cities, towns and places overrun with people, the Earth's energy gets suppressed beneath the surface due to humanity's lack of awareness. But here, in the vast expanse of the arctic tundra, it was right on the surface. And it was strong. It felt as if Chevron Mountain was ready to open up and literally speak at any moment. The spirit of the mountain was fully present and very alive.

Jason didn't see any outcrops on his hike across the tundra expanse to the ridge. It was all covered in glacial till. However, as he started his several hundred foot climb up to the ridge, he literally stumbled over the first rock. It caught his attention. It was a sedimentary rock like so many others in the area. However, this one had a little quartz vein that was rimmed with beautiful hues of green and blue. They were the minerals azurite and malachite, colors of rusted out copper. Jason quickly pulled out his hand lens and gave it a closer look. Upon inspection, he could see tiny flecks of native copper. It looked promising, so he took a sample and threw it in his backpack.

As he continued his climb up to the ridge line, he noticed more rocks with copper showings, lying right on the surface. They were increasing in number the higher he climbed. He guessed a quartz outcrop with native copper could be exposed on the ridge.

When he reached the ridge top, he stopped to surveyed the scenery. His spirit and intellect were both deeply engaged in that magnificent moment. The vastness of the tundra was utterly breathtaking and Chevron Mountain, now very close in the east, was radiating a spiritual splendor.

The sedimentary rocks on the ridge were tilted up, running north and south, perpendicular to the ridge line. As Jason walked toward Chevron Mountain, he would be crossing various sediment layers. He saw intermittent outcrops dotting the ridge, so he headed for the first one. When he arrived, he saw a small bleb of a quartz vein with a little copper staining. It was certainly nothing to get excited about but it was something. As he pulled out a sample bag to take a sample, he glanced up the ridge. He did a double-take in disbelief. There was a copper-rich quartz vein, about a foot wide, going right up the ridge toward Chevron Mountain. "Wow," he thought out loud, "I didn't see that a minute ago. It seemed like it appeared right in front of me."

As he continued up the ridge, following the vein, he took samples about every 100 feet. However, as luck would have it, a very unnerving fog began to blow in from the south. Not only was it cutting off his view to the tundra valley below, it was also making it difficult to see the mineralization on the ridge. Cautiously, he continued his trek, as the vein disappeared and reappeared in the fog. It was eerie. Adding to the mystique, was the view of Chevron Mountain, poking through a hole in the clouds. It's intimidating grandeur was the only thing untouched by the fog.

The mountain's cliff face was now only about 100 hundred yards away. At the top of the ridge where it met the mountain was a flat moraine, about 100 feet long by 50 feet wide. It was a remnant from a glacier melted long ago. To Jason, it looked like an enormous park bench for a giant. Squinting his eyes and focusing just above the moraine, he saw the quartz vein in the face of the cliff. It was cutting through the pushed up sedimentary layers of Chevron Mountain.

After a short but vigorous scramble up to flat ground, Jason immediately started to feel dizzy. With his head in a spin, he thought, "Whoa, what is up? Must be vertigo from the clouds… Can't see the valley…Or maybe I got some bad mayo in my sandwich…Man…somethin' ain't right." It took a few moments to steady himself and catch his wind.

With a head full of dizzy, he sauntered over to take a look at the vein in the cliff face. It was nearly 12 inches wide. It was comprised of native copper and milky white quartz, with neon green and blue copper rust. It was a magnificent sight for someone exploring for minerals.

About 10 feet above his head, the vein cut through a sediment layer made of pure iron. The iron stood out because, unlike the surrounding gray rock, it weathered to a deep maroon-red. Jason's eyes almost popped out of his head when he saw the intersection between the iron layer and the copper vein. It was a magnificent crystal over 18 inches tall and six inches wide, nestled in a small grotto. Jason's strong suit wasn't mineralogy, so he wasn't sure what it was. "It's not quartz. Barite? Topaz? Certainly not diamond." Its unique placement in the cliff made it seem like a sacred icon for all to see. Never in all his geologic explorations had he seen anything so magnificent. He was so in awe, he took a few steps back, sat down and just stared.

Within a few minutes, the clouds framed a hole in the sky, just large enough for a ray of sunlight to shoot through. It landed directly on the crystal like a spotlight. The crystal lit up like a Christmas tree, reflecting every color of the rainbow straight at Jason. Immediately, his dizziness mushroomed, his head started to pound, and he was overcome with nausea to the point of vomiting. He rolled over on his hands and knees as the crystalline light show continued. He felt like he was getting poisoned with radiation. Rolling back over, he tried to sit up as his eyesight unexpectedly began to waver. He saw translucent images, vague silhouettes of people, three-dimensional geometric shapes and symbols. A flurry of overlapping activity was happening at the same time and in the same place. He felt like he was peering through a window into a different dimension.

It was so bizarre. Jason had no idea what was happening. All he knew for sure was that it was too intense. He couldn't take it. So he crawled down off the glacial bench with his backpack, tried to regain some normalcy, and prepared to radio for the helicopter.

Because it was cloudy, Jason would need GPS coordinates to relay his position to the pilot. When he pulled out his GPS unit and turned it on, the batteries were dead. "How could that be?" he thought, "I charged those damn things all night. Hmm, maybe I didn't have the charger plugged in all the way." It was a good thing he carried a backup for such emergencies. It was an old-school Brunton compass. Those babies were precision instruments from a geologist's time gone by, back when geology was an art form. As he steadied his Brunton and pointed east to get a bearing on Chevron Mountain, the compass needle went nuts. It started swinging back and forth in wild disarray and even spun in complete circles a few times. Jason thought, "Great. Maybe the banded iron is throwing off the compass magnetics…Or maybe it's the whole weirdness to this place…An arctic Bermuda Triangle…I'll never get a bearing up here. This mountain is crazy. I'll have to walk back to where I started."

Shaky and unnerved, Jason radioed the chopper pilot. However, the pilot was temporarily pinned down by cloud cover. Due to the fog, he wouldn't be able to land on Jason's ridge either. They'd have to meet back where Jason was dropped off, a few miles away. It took him another couple of hours to get there. Thirty minutes after that, they were flying back to camp.

Jason didn't dare mention a thing to the pilot. How could he explain what happened? No one would believe him. It was too overwhelming to fathom, let alone explain. He tried to steady himself and assemble the events of the day in his head. "C'mon man, pull yourself together," he said under his breath. "Don't let this run away with you." He desperately wanted to get a grip on himself because he still had one day left in the arctic.

Back at camp, everyone was abuzz. The geology foreman said as soon as the samples were ready to ship and all the gear was packed and ready to load, everyone could have the last day off to do as they pleased…complete with helicopter shuttles. It was a perk for three weeks of a collective job well done. Everyone was excited. It was a no brainer the crew would be in full swing packing things up after dinner.

It was well before bedtime when the camp was packed up. As soon as the last box was placed in the staging area, the entire crew met in the mess tent to plan the last day's events. The geology foreman and three other geologists were going to spend the day fishing a stretch of river they'd been scoping out for the past three weeks. The helicopter pilot would join them in between shuttles. Jason's field partner was going to spend the day in meditation on top of the tallest peak in the field area. The camp cook Bea and the helicopter mechanic were going to get out and hike. They'd been imprisoned in camp for three weeks and couldn't wait to get out on the tundra.

And Jason? He'd regained his composure and wanted to head straight back to the bench below Chevron Mountain. He wouldn't rest until the mystery of the day's events had been solved.

Chapter 3
Visions

Sleepless
That night, Jason couldn't get to sleep. He tossed and turned in his sleeping bag trying to make sense of the occurrences over the past few weeks. He knew there was some enormous spiritual power on and around Chevron Mountain. But what did it all mean? He knew there had to be some deeper significance. Hopefully, his return trip to the mountain would solve the riddle.

Jason was no stranger to spirituality. In fact, it was his first love. Before he came to the arctic, he immersed himself in literature about shamanism and the mysteries of the far north. For him, this expedition was just as much a search for his soul as it was for precious metals. He longed to experience a deeper connection with the Great Spirit of the Land.

Jason's passion for mystical experience had elevated to a burning desire by the time he wandered up Chevron Mountain. He was fully aware there were locations on the planet referred to as Power Centers, Portals and Vortexes. They were supposedly specific locations that carried highly charged Earth energies. He'd even been to a few minor ones. However, nowhere in his travels had he ever experienced anything close to the energetic magnitude of Chevron Mountain. He admitted quite plainly to himself, he was deeply intimidated by the mountain's power. The possibility of disorienting or even dangerous spiritual experiences loomed heavily in the front of his mind. However, he knew this was a once-in-a-lifetime opportunity and he wouldn't miss it for anything, come what may. And he only had one day left to do it.

Still unable to sleep, Jason's mind continued to re-work his incredible experiences in the arctic. He suspected his many encounters with wildlife were visitations from totem animals. Plus, their message must have been significant because the encounters were so powerful and unusual. As he continued to toss and turn, he pondered the possible meanings to the signs and messages they were trying to convey.

"Bears," he thought, as he rolled over onto his shoulder. "Aren't bear totems suppose to represent spiritual power and protection? The gigantic Bubba Bear that went straight for Bea's brownies must indicate massive power and protection around Chevron Mountain. They're hibernators too…masters of the subconscious dream world. Maybe ol' Chevron is a gateway to a powerful dream world, like the stories of Don Juan in books written by Carlos Castaneda."

As his mind raced along, he flipped back over to his other side. "But an aborted bear fetus? How weird is that?" Just the thought of it triggered a flash of fairly strong guilt. However, Jason considered guilt to be one of the most useless emotions in the human experience. For him, it usually meant he was not taking responsibility for something. So he set his guilt aside and continued to muse over the grizzly fetus. He thought it was an obvious sign of enormous spiritual potential, just waiting to grow. He wasn't sure if the fetus represented the mountain, him or both. "Maybe I'll find out tomorrow," he thought.

He rolled on to his back and shifted his thoughts to the wolves. "Three white wolves with two dead caribou, displaying a demeanor of contented, selfless pride." That encounter was beyond his mental grasp. There were way too many signals that could be read into that one. Still he kicked it around in his head. "Wolves represent spiritual protection in the context of community and family. The dead caribou?…Abundance. There were three of them too…hmm…The Holy Trinity from Christianity?…Arts and communication from Numerology?…White represents purity and holiness?…Ahhh…I dunno…I could over-think this to death… Maybe I just need to let it go." With that final thought, he closed his eyes, rolled over and drifted off into a very restless sleep.

That night, he dreamt he was devoured by a giant bear and a pack of white wolves.

After breakfast the following morning, it was decided. Since Jason's location was the furthest from camp, the pilot wanted to do the longest flight first. However, truth be told, he wanted to drop the fishermen off last. That way, he could pile out with them and get first crack at a prime fishing spot.

It was about a 30 minute flight to the north, from camp to Chevron Mountain. As the chopper made a beeline toward the peak, emerging in the autumn arctic morning was the glacial bench on the peak's western flank.

"Right there," Jason said to the pilot, pointing to the flat patch of ground at the base of the cliff.

As the pilot slowed his blades on descent, he stopped in mid-air about 50 feet above the bench. Controlled but perplexed, the pilot shot Jason a glance of mild bewilderment.

He said, "I can't put her down. The air pressure's not right. Feels like opposite ends of a magnet."

Without blinking an eye or giving it a second thought, he pulled the helicopter back, flew about a half mile down the ridge, and set it down. It was only a few hundred feet away from where Jason ascended the ridge the day before.

The pilot looked at Jason and commanded, "I'll see you right here at 4:00 sharp," as he punched the coordinates into his GPS unit.

Jason nodded and hopped out, grabbed his gear, knelt on the ground, and gave a thumbs up. The pilot nodded back, pulled on his joystick, lifted his bird into the air, and slowly evaporated into the southern horizon.

As Jason assembled his gear he thought, "That was strange. There's not a breath of wind. Why couldn't he set the chopper down? The mechanic gave the bird its routine maintenance yesterday. It's good to go. Huh…Air pressure's not right?…Opposite ends of a magnet? I've never heard a pilot say that before. Oh well, at least he didn't seem too concerned. Maybe the banded iron formation is causing a magnetic anomaly on the bench…or maybe it's a vortex…or a portal…or…something else." There was a knot starting to tighten up in Jason's stomach. He was having second thoughts about re-visiting Chevron Mountain.

Return of the King
Jason anxiously began his trek back up the ridge to follow the vein toward Chevron Mountain. Several hundred feet ahead was the first outcrop with copper showings he discovered the day before. With a tinge of gold rush fever, he walked straight over to where he took his first sample.

Much to his surprise, he couldn't find it. Quizzically, he searched all over the outcrop. There was no chipped rock from where he pounded his hammer on the bedrock the day before. There was no blue and green copper rust. It was just plain gray sedimentary bedrock. "Funny," he thought. "Must be the wrong outcrop. I could have sworn it was this one. Oh well, outcrops have a way of looking the same. Plus, the sun was at a different angle yesterday. Must be casting some different shadows." However, as he looked the outcrop over again, he thought for sure it was the same one. But he'd been disoriented in the field before. All he could do was shrug his shoulders.

Jason swung around. As he fixed his gaze toward the mountain, he saw the familiar pattern of outcrops he'd seen less than 24 hours earlier. "There," he said to himself. "Over there. There's that four-foot high blocky outcrop with distinct layers. I remember that one. A six-inch wide copper-quartz vein cuts right through the center of it."

With a hurried step, he made his way over to the solid stack of rock. Again, no vein. No copper, no quartz, no green and blue stain…nothing, just ordinary gray rock. "Am I in the right place?" he began to second-guess himself. Looking east he thought, "No…there's Chevron Mountain…this is the western ridge… there's the bench…and the cliff. This is insane! Am I going out of my mind?"

Astonished and with a growing feeling of uneasiness, he continued his march up the ridge toward the glacial bench. Murmuring to himself he said, "How can a vein of solid copper and quartz just disappear? I took samples. They're hard proof. I'll pull them out when I get back to camp." Then he remembered the samples were being flown out of camp as he spoke. A Twin Otter bush plane was scheduled to arrive that morning to pick up the rock samples and the first round of supplies. The samples were gone.

His heart immediately sank. Something was not at all right. It was the same feeling he'd had when he discovered he was once the victim of a financial scam. He felt exceedingly vulnerable. Except the pranksters in this scam were spirits from a different dimension. Was this a joke or would he never be seen or heard from again? A tingle of fear rocketed straight up his spine and settled in the center of his chest. Unsuccessfully trying to control his fear, he wondered, "Oh my God, what have I gotten myself into?"

Jason took a very deep breath and rustled up as much courage as he could to continue up the ridge. He kept repeating to himself, "Fear is only fear. It's only a smoke screen. Just step through it. Just step through it." Determined, he kept slowly pushing himself on. With each outcrop he passed and recognized, he saw there were no veins anywhere. The mineralization was gone…vanished…vamoosed.

When he was within a hundred yards of the bench, a light wind kicked up and fog started to form, just like the day before. Jason, in a mounting fear that was nearing hysteria, screamed from the tops of his lungs at the mountain, "C'mon!...Clouds again!?! This is starting to look like a bad horror movie!...Is that the best you can do?!?" Within a few eerie minutes, the wind died down and the clouds silently dissipated. Apparently, the mystical and foreboding mountain had a sense of humor.

The Portal
As Jason pulled himself up onto the glacial bench, he wasn't surprised to discover the vein and crystal were no longer in the cliff face. He took a few steps to get a closer look and immediately began to feel dizzy and nauseated again. Unconsciously, he steadied himself and took and internal assessment. While he was focusing on his unexpected sickness, he saw something like heat waves forming in front of him. They were blurring his view of Chevron Mountain's cliff face.

As he tried to focus his gaze through the translucent cloud, he noticed it looked roughly like the Northern Lights. It was a clear, semi-transparent area of light that looked like pleated curtains in a window. It seemed electrical. It was also in constant motion. The edges were vague but the entire mirage looked about 15 feet high and about 30 feet across. It wasn't much bigger than the mess tent back at camp.

Attempting to quell his faint queasiness, Jason stared in amazement as the Portal continued to take shape. He could barely make out the fuzzy cliff face of Chevron Mountain on the other side. However, one thing he could see for sure was an enormous amount of activity going on inside. He saw flashes of light and what looked liked images of people. And there were clouds of color darting all over the place. Furthermore, what Jason couldn't see, he could feel. He sensed an energy that felt like a cross between electricity and radiation, emanating off its surface. He thought if he reached out to touch it, he'd be zapped like an electric fence. Oddly, he wasn't surprised or afraid. He was more in a cautious and deep state of awe, like a kid at a carnival. He could have stood and stared at it for hours.

The Elder
As the activity on the inside of the Portal continued to increase, Jason saw the image of what looked like a man coming in and out of focus. The image quickly formed and as soon as Jason fixed his gaze on it, it faded from view. Over the next few minutes, the image appeared and disappeared several times. To Jason, the ambiance of his aura was unmistakable.

He was an Inuit Elder, a native from the shores of the Arctic Ocean. Wrapped in seal skin and polar bear fur, he was exuding a transcendental presence of calm, joy and acceptance that only a spiritual master can. In the same moment, he conveyed the self-assurance of an ancient shamanic sage and the purity of an innocent child. He reminded Jason of the character Ootek from one of his favorite movies, *Never Cry Wolf*. The mere sight of him humbled Jason into a deep state of reverence. After fading in and out of view several more times, the Elder finally took on the form of a physical human being. He gestured softly to Jason by waving his hand toward himself and in the gentlest of voices said, "Come… please."

Jason responded to the invitation by throwing up a wall of internal resistance. He froze in his tracks. However, the Elder's presence engulfed Jason in an aura of unconditional love, melting away anything that resembled fear. Jason felt a lightness consume his body and he thought he was floating. It felt like the Elder was magnetically pulling him closer. But as he looked down, he could see his legs and feet were walking.

Jason was in a deep trance as he passed through the Portal's exterior. However, instead of being zapped, he felt his body pulse, as if he were walking through a weightless breaking surf on an endless beach in paradise. It was oddly electric, yet not, at the same time. There was no doubt he was drifting into an altered, yet heightened, state of awareness. His entire perception of the physical world was rapidly shifting into a dream-like quality. He felt like he no longer had a physical body but only a wispy, dreamy resemblance. He was also relieved to notice his dizziness and nausea had vanished.

Jason looked around and studied the Portal. From the inside, the boundaries were opaque and indistinct. He could see outside. Chevron Mountain and the tundra valley below were visible but nebulous, somewhat like looking underwater. There was also a flurry of activity. There were constantly moving energies, colors, geometric shapes and an endless array of images. It seemed as if thoughts were constantly manifesting as images, only to vanish as quickly as they appeared.

Jason stared on in amazement at the mystical psychedelic light show, captivated by an overwhelming sense of tranquility. All of his concerns, cares and worries over the course of his entire life, suddenly became entirely meaningless. Without judgment, he recognized his values in life had mostly been off target. Now, all he wanted was peace. So he opened his heart and allowed himself to absorb it like a sponge.

The Inuit Elder was now, more or less, in constant focus. He was standing directly in front of Jason, in the exact center of the Portal. Jason sensed a message was forthcoming. Slowly, the Elder began to speak to Jason in what he assumed was some dialect of Inuit. His voice was soft but strong and clear. However, Jason had no idea how he was able to understand the Elder because he did not physically move his mouth and Jason didn't speak Inuit.

Please don't be frightened, the Elder began. *I am here as part of your own co-creation with the Great Spirit. This day signifies the beginning of your karmic path, an agreement you made with yourself before entering this life. It is yours and yours alone to fulfill. Today, you will be given visions of your spirit guides and helpers. They are your teachers. It is your destiny to meet each of them in your physical life. Each teacher will convey a universal spiritual truth. You, in turn, must learn and assimilate each truth into your being. This will allow you to pass the truths along to others, aiding them in their soul evolution. However, you must understand, it is absolutely necessary for you to engage and activate these truths within yourself first. Only then, will you be able to assist others.*

The way you have chosen will not be easy. You will be required to utilize and strengthen your will. However, as you take necessary action, you will receive enormous help from your angels and guides. The Great Spirit will also be forever at your side. I highly encourage you to invoke Its help regularly.

This is your quest. I wish you well.

Vision - The Octahedron
With his last invisible breath, the Inuit Elder faded from view. What was left in his wake were platonic solids and proportioned dimensional reality, also known as sacred geometry.

Jason was instantly transported into a world he did not know. This was a dimension far beyond his familiar limitations of the 3D physical world. It was a realm of swirling color and geometric shapes of light, drifting through a void darker than he'd ever known. Delicately floating and endlessly spinning, they continually combined in different assemblages, then separated, creating a perpetual exchange and release of energy. As Jason observed in wonderment, he surmised the shapes were actual living creatures. However, they came from an existence far beyond the Earth-plane he called home.

Life in this dimension was more basic, more fundamentally connected to its spiritual center. These were the energetic building blocks of life itself. Each spinning geometric shape radiated the essence of individual virtues, such as compassion, forgiveness, self-acceptance, gratitude, patience, self-confidence, and loyalty. There were thousands of them, some far beyond the comprehension of human experience, expressed in the floating and spinning forms of pyramids, spheres and perfectly shaped 3D polygons. Collectively, they radiated a vibration of pure unconditional love.

Jason was mesmerized. He could feel energy being emitted, as the images passed by. Somehow, he understood the shapes contained encrypted information to aid in human development. He even recognized some of the geometric patterns, which had already been gifted to humanity: the Great Pyramids, Stonehenge, numerous temples, and crop circles. Jason guessed those sacred structures contained beneficial energy that surpassed human comprehension, even though many were crafted by human hands.

As a geologist, Jason also recognized that many of the floating shapes were identical to the crystal structures of minerals, the fundamental building blocks of planet Earth. At that instant, a light of illumination flashed through Jason's mind. He suddenly *knew* something he'd felt his entire life. The Earth is sacred. Not only because it's the source of life and our home, but because of its nature, its pure essence. The planet's fundamental building blocks are images formed by Divine thought, intention and energy.

Jason immediately became overrun with an anguishing mental conflict. "How has humanity evolved to be agents of destruction on their own sacred planet, their own home? Look at me. I'm a geologist searching for the next open pit mine in the Arctic wilderness. How has it come to this? Aren't human beings composed of the same Divine building blocks as the Earth? How can we destroy something that is essentially us? What went wrong?"

Before he gave himself permission to get lost in that endless self-inflicted debate, a particular image drifted in his direction. It stopped about half an arm's length away, centered at eye-level. It was a slowly spinning gold translucent octahedron, demanding his attention. It was contained by a barely visible sphere of pure platinum light, also spinning but in the opposite direction.

Jason was very familiar with this image. It came to him in a vision when he was in college, experimenting with psychotropic stimulants. That experience was so powerful, he never forgot it. It was his first experience of what he called God. Etched in the permanent recesses of his memory, he remembered it as formidable, authentic, and true, even if it was drug induced.

Awed by the return of an old and dear friend, Jason locked onto the octahedron with undivided attention. It radiated an invisible beam of energy, straight into his forehead through his third-eye. He knew the shape was communicating in a language far beyond the limitation of human linguistics.

Initially alarmed, Jason soon realized the energy wasn't harmful but extremely life enhancing. Enraptured in euphoria, he saw an endless parade of other-worldly glyphs and symbols streaming into his third eye. He guessed they were encoded messages that would trigger at developmental stages in his life, assisting him in his earthly mission.

Jason drank the energy up like a parched camel in an oasis. He soaked it in until his energetic and physical bodies were about to explode. Then, the octahedron slowly drifted back into the blackness. Jason lay back and effortlessly watched countless other geometric images dance across the Portal. All the while, his body continued to tingle and vibrate, from infused energy assimilating into his system.

In the pitch blackness above, Jason watched the eternal ballet of the geometric shapes. They combined to form galaxies, nebulae, and solar systems. Then they exploded, releasing raw creative power back into the darkness, just to begin the whole business over again. It was a continual regenerative process of birth, life and death. It was the story of the Universe, creating and destroying itself, over and over and over. It was beautiful beyond description. A beauty that lulled Jason into a deep and peaceful sleep.

Reorienting
When Jason awoke, he slowly reconnoitered himself and wondered how long he'd been out. All he knew for sure was that it was still daylight. However, a thick fog had moved in during his

slumber. So he began the task of finding his bearings. It seemed he was still on the glacial bench below Chevron Mountain. Only much to his grateful surprise, the translucent Portal was gone.

Jason was enormously relieved to be out from under the grip of the Portal and its intense visions. All he wanted to do now was go back home. However, he had no idea how much time had passed, or if he was even still in the same century. As that notion dawned on him, he suddenly felt completely alone. If he could only find his backpack and radio. He began scurrying about, frantically searching in the dense fog. But because the fog was so thick, he couldn't walk more than a few steps in any direction without becoming completely disoriented. He was totally lost on a patch of ground less than half the size of a football field.

The Prophecy
When Jason finally realized he was wandering around in circles, he stopped and tried to collect himself. As he steadied himself into a forced state of calm, he furrowed his brow and stared in wonder at what appeared to be a hooded figure approaching through the mist. All he could think was, "Is it another vision? Gawd, I hope not."

No. The Inuit Elder had returned. He advanced toward Jason, as if floating on a cloud, and stopped a few feet away. With a slight squint in his eyes and a faint grin, he revealed the wisdom of ancientness. He proceeded to speak in the gentlest of tones and said, *"Now you have met your first guide. Many more are on the way. They will assist you on your journey of soul evolution. They will introduce themselves to you in visions and dreams before they appear in your physical world."*

At that moment the Elder stopped speaking. Appearing next to him were ghost-like apparitions of people that came in and out of view. First was the octahedron followed immediately by what looked like an East Indian Yogi. Next was a husband a wife Hindu couple. Following them were two Madonnas that reminded

Jason on the Virgin Mary. A Polynesian Goddess appeared next and then a Native American Indian Chief.

They continued to appear and dissolve for a very long time until Jason had their images etched firmly into the hard drive of his brain.

When they finally faded from view, the Elder continued, *"Do not try to find them, for they are as mysterious as the wind. They will be revealed to you as your path in life naturally unfolds. You will find them through signs and memories that have been created on this day. Some may even appear to you in the flesh. After you meet them, ask for their help often, for they are with you always.*

"Go in faith. May your heart be strong. When we meet again, your journey will be complete."

Back to Camp
With his timeless grin, the Elder turned and vanished into the fog. Soon after, a hole opened in the clouds, serving as the perfect window for the approaching helicopter, as it prepared its descent to the landing zone. Jason quickly found his backpack because the helicopter nearly landed on it. Hunkered over, he ran to the chopper and grabbed his pack, under the deafening wash of its rotating blades. Trying not to hurry, in the midst of an adrenaline infused helicopter pick up, he flung the door open, tossed in his pack, and climbed aboard.

"Sorry I'm late," the pilot jeered with a cocky laugh. "The fishin' was incredible…like shootin' fish in a barrel. We probably caught a hundred of 'em. We even kept a couple to prove we're not total liars. How 'bout you?"

Jason flashed him a speechless thumbs up. That was the best he could come up with, seeing how he was still in a state of shock. The last thing he wanted to do was talk. His mind only had enough energy to think of what might lie ahead. He knew he would be scouring the depth of his memory banks in the weeks to come, in a desperate attempt to piece together the events of this unreal day. But for now, he was exhausted.

When they lifted off, Jason saw they were right where he was dropped off earlier, about a half mile west of Chevron Mountain. "How the hell did I get here?" he thought. "I thought I was at the base of the mountain on the glacial bench?"

As the helicopter peeled away toward camp, Jason switched off his headset and forced himself to sleep.

When Jason arrived at camp, everyone was in an upbeat buzz, sharing tales of adventures, wildlife sightings, and the big one that got away. As he slowly slogged out of the helicopter, he exchanged a few brief pleasantries with his colleagues and went straight to the utility tent. He couldn't socialize. He was too tired and his mind was swirling at a million miles per hour. Withdrawal was the only thing that made sense.

When he entered the utility tent, he locked the door, quickly undressed, left his clothes scatted on the floor, and tumbled into the shower. He braced himself against the shower wall, hung his head, and let the hot water run until the tent was completely filled with steam. He had absolutely no desire to move. It was everything he could muster to dry off, get dressed, and wander over to the mess tent where he had to interact briefly before bed.

The next day, the entire crew flew back to Anchorage. Jason had four weeks left to fulfill the terms of his seasonal contract. He still had to compile a season's worth of data, write a couple of reports, and complete a small field project about 50 miles west.

For lodging, he was holed up in a motel room in beautiful downtown Spenard, sandwiched between Anchorage's business district and the airport. Over the next month, he found it almost impossible to focus on his work. His mind was constantly distracted (i.e. obsessed) with the events of Chevron Mountain. It took every ounce of focus to complete the final report.

Each evening, he locked himself in his motel room with a take-out tray of sushi and tired to recall, in detail, that mystical day in the Portal. Over and over, he reflected on the apparition of the octahedron and the visions of his guides. He also wrote for hours on end and drew sketches from memory, until his notebook was overflowing with information and images. But more than anything, he wanted to remember the sequence in which his guides would appear:

Octahedron
Yogi
Hindus
Madonnas
Goddess
Chief
Elder

If anyone ever thumbed through his scattered memoirs, they'd quickly come to the conclusion this was the stuff of someone deeply disturbed, if not flat-out psychotic. Jason realized that potential and vowed to keep his chronicles private, at least until he left Alaska.

Chapter 4
Pain

It didn't take long for the Anchorage sky to turn steely gray and dust the surrounding mountains with their first covering of snow. It was October. The Alaskan winter had arrived and it was time for Jason to go home.

Washington State. Not a bad place to call home. Salt water, mountains, loads of evergreens and fresh air. He liked it and was glad to be back. However, as he settled in, Jason was surprised; he found it difficult to care about anything. So little mattered. He didn't give a rip about what kind of car he drove, owning a house, or beefing up an investment portfolio. Those illusions just seemed to drive the rats crazy in their endless, insatiable race. After what he'd been through, he found he could no longer relate to society as a whole. In the few months he was gone, it seemed the entire world had gone mad. But it was just the same as before he left. "Maybe something else changed," he thought. "Maybe…it was me."

Jason's major problem was that he'd just been on a world-class expedition. Flying in helicopters all summer in the Alaskan outback, topped with phenomenal mystical experiences, was nothing short of going to the moon. He felt like Frodo Baggins returning to the Shire after destroying Mordor to save Middle-earth. Somehow, Jason had graduated into the elite category of *Genuine Adventurer*, now in the esteemed company of predecessors, such as Sir Ernest Shackleton and Dr. Livingstone. Therefore, as soon as he arrived back home, he dutifully adhered to their tradition and fell into a deep depression. The Shire no longer made sense. The only sensible thing to do was start planning his next adventure.

The Next Adventure
About two weeks later, Jason was lying on the couch with his first season's bout of seasonal mood disorder. There was a low-flying

dark cloud parked in the middle of his forehead, sucking the life force out of his cerebral cortex. He was in the midst of forcing himself off the couch, in a feeble attempt to avoid succumbing to the blackness. Suddenly, the front door flung open with an accompanying blast of frigid air. It was his roommate Jonathan.

"You're home early," Jason moaned, as he slowly rolled up.

"Get used to it," Jonathan snapped back. "I just got laid off."

"Wow, man. Bummer. Sorry to hear that. You okay?"

"Ah, forget it," Jonathan replied. "I hated that place anyway. C'mon, get up. Let's go out for coffee."

The ensuing conversation in the coffee shop turned out to be the brainstorming session of a lifetime. Jason listened to Jonathan's woes of working as a car mechanic, in a shop run by an imbecile. Jason, on the other hand, spilled the beans about his experiences on Chevron Mountain for the very first time.

Jonathan had his own spiritual inclinations and was an informal student on the teachings of Gurdjieff. When he heard Jason's visions of Elders, spiritual masters and sacred symbols, his wheels really started turning. "We need to find out what these visions mean," he eagerly campaigned.

"We???" Jason responded in defense. "Did you ever stop to think these experiences might be meant for me alone?" He was very sensitive and unsure of what he'd gone through. The notion crossed his mind more that once that maybe he was going crazy. He felt very vulnerable and didn't want to expose his experiences to anybody.

"No way!" Jonathan shot back. "This is major stuff. Humanity is on the verge of a massive awakening. Don't you think this could be part of it?"

"Whoa, boy," Jason commanded. "Not so fast. I'm open to the idea of looking into the meaning behind what happened but let's leave the rest of the human race out of it."

"Okay, okay," Jonathan said, as he backed off. "But there are places in the world where people know about this kind of stuff. Ya know, like spiritual centers of enlightenment. I've been reading about a bunch of them lately. Most of 'em are outside the US."

Now, he had Jason's attention. He replied, "Oh yeah? Like where?"

"There's a bunch in India and a real cool one in northern Scotland. It's an international spiritual community called the Findhorn Foundation. It's been going strong for a couple of decades. Apparently, there have been numerous miracles and awakenings reported there. Plus, they have a magical garden and they offer all sorts of classes and workshops. I bet somebody will know something there."

"Findhorn, ya say?" Jason mused out loud. "Hmm...Scotland? How much money you got?"

"Enough," Jonathan shrugged.

Without a breath of time for a second thought, Jason energetically exclaimed, "Hell, let's go!"

Findhorn
Two weeks later, our heroes were in Heathrow International, trying to figure out how to get to northern Scotland. They rented a car and in the "Learn Quick or Die School of Driving," they quickly adjusted to driving on the wrong side of the road.

It was a long straight shot to northern Scotland. The open landscape lived up to its Braveheart reputation, as it was continuously cleansed by endless squalls from foreboding Scottish skies. Scotland seemed like one gigantic green sponge.

When they arrived on the grounds of Findhorn, they were required to take a brief guided tour and listen to a presentation on the history and mission of the Findhorn Foundation. That's where they were introduced to the magic of Scottish story telling.

At the end of the presentation, everyone filtered out of the auditorium, except Jason, Jonathan and one other lone wolf. He was a German named Hans, traveling about on holiday. The three of them struck up an instant fraternity and decided to room together in a caravan, on the east side of campus. Jonathan was chomping at the bit to begin the exploration of discovering the meaning behind Jason's visions. Jason was way more apprehensive. And Hans, of course, had no idea what he was getting himself into.

*

The daily routine at the Findhorn revolved around community meals. Jason thought it was a beautiful way to live. Each meal was a celebration of the spirituality and unity the Findhorn Foundation stood for. However, suppertime didn't magically happen all by itself.

Guests at Findhorn were required to contribute. In exchange, they received a reduced rate for their lodging. There were three basic work choices. You could work in the bountiful gardens, help in the kitchen, or assist in general maintenance and cleaning. Jason was all in for outdoor work, so he chose the gardens. Jonathan, the mechanic, thought he could best put his skills to use in maintenance. Hans opted for the kitchen. Each of them hoped their chosen work area would bring a famous Findhorn miracle.

That night, as they were lounging around the caravan and sipping tea, Jonathan could no longer contain his enthusiasm. "Man, I can't wait to start picking the brains of some of the people around here. Do you think there's a secret society of mystics here? Maybe somebody has a direct link to extraterrestrial intelligence. This is where were gonna find out that Jason's visions are part of a revolutionary shift in global consciousness."

Hans was busily trying to mentally translate all the blather that was shooting out of Jonathan's mouth. When he looked at Jason for assistance, Jason just rolled his eyes and shook his head, as if to say, "Don't bother."

However, Hans was too intrigued. He thought he was missing out on something important and asked, "What are you guys talking about?"

Over the next several hours, Jason and Jonathan revealed the purpose behind their mission to Findhorn. Hans listened intently with widened eyes behind John Lennon spectacles. This type of surrealism was way off his personal radar but he was intently interested. Adventures of this magnitude didn't come along every day. For Hans the world traveler, this was another chance to satisfy his insatiable wanderlust, another pin to stick in his wall map of the world.

*

The next morning at breakfast, Jonathan announced an interesting flyer he saw to an upcoming workshop. "Looks like there's a fascinating event called Holotropic Breathwork this weekend. Apparently, it's being put on by some well-known guy from Switzerland. Wanna go?"

"I dunno. What is it again?" Jason inquired, as Hans nodded inquisitively.

"It's an all-day meditation with a lot of music. It's gonna be in the music studio behind the auditorium. Plus, it's only 35 pounds. Could be very other-worldly."

"Sounds great to me," Jason replied. "When is it?"

"Saturday," Jonathan said.

"Bummer," Hans chimed in, proud to display his newly learned English slang. "I'll be meeting my girlfriend in Wales next weekend."

"Okay, I guess it's just me and you," Jason said, looking at Jonathan. "I"ll pay for it today at the office, on my way over to the gardens. Looks like we'll be here at least through the weekend."

With that decision made, the three partners split up and ventured off to their respective work areas.

*

After purchasing tickets for the workshop, Jason sauntered over to the central greenhouse to meet the supervisor and receive his work detail. When he arrived at the designated time of 9:00 sharp, no one was there. He stood around and waited for a very uncomfortable five minutes and wondered if he was in the right location. Just as he was about to leave and go ask around, a thin, saintly-looking woman, wearing knee-high rubber boots, floated in and acknowledged Jason as if he were a very pleasant afterthought.

"Oh…hello. My name is Ula," she said in a strong Dutch accent. "Are you here to work in the garden today?" Jason self-consciously nodded and introduced himself. "Marvelous," she replied. "Let's wait a few more minutes and see who else shows up. Would you like some tea?" Jason politely declined and Ula looked at him somewhat puzzled. Then she reminded herself that he was an American and he probably didn't recognize the magic of teatime (which came quite frequently at Findhorn).

It didn't take Jason long to figure out, life at Findhorn didn't operate under the push of corporate time tables he was accustomed to when he worked as a geologist. It was totally laid back, something completely foreign to him. However, he quickly learned to appreciate the groove.

Within 15 minutes, the rest of the crew arrived on "Findhorn Time." There was Vasudeva, an impish, free-spirited jester from Russia. Anne, a frail and deeply disturbed, psychic woman from Ireland. And Sergio. He was a seemingly normal college-aged kid from Spain.

After the novelty of being on an international gardening crew evaporated, the gang got down to brass tacks…removing sod to expand the southern end of the gardens. Jason dove in with sparks flying off his pick and shovel, vigorously attacking the task at hand. He was proud to show off his well-trained American work ethic. However, it didn't take him long to learn, based on the facial expressions of his workmates, he was working way too hard. Not knowing any better, he just shrugged his shoulders and kept on plugging away, ignorant to the diminished demands of a more refined culture.

Jason was about ready to break into his first well-earned manly sweat when he heard, "Yoo-hoo! Yoo-hoo!" It was Ula. "Teatime!" she hollered with delight.

"Already?" Jason could barely believe. "I just got started."

Nevertheless, despite his inner capitalistic rumblings, Ula's much-welcomed invocation caught everyone's undivided attention. Without the utterance of another word, everyone hung up their tools and promptly scattered like cockroaches.

*

Jason wandered over to the coffeehouse, near the auditorium. When he arrived, he couldn't believe his eyes. The place was packed. "Wow, doesn't anybody work around here?" he thought to himself. From one quick look around, he could immediately tell this was where all the action in Findhorn went down.

It was buzzing with activity, filled with very unconventional people from all over the world. Most of the patrons looked fairly normal but Jason knew this crowd was comprised of gurus, psychics, mystics, shamans, healers and caretakers of the planet. Collectively, they had a very unique vibe. You could just feel it. Furthermore, almost everyone was engrossed in deep, heartfelt discussion.

As he scanned the morass hoping to find an available seat, Jason saw a hand shoot skyward and wave to get his attention. It was Hans, on break from the kitchen. He arrived before the rush and saved a table, hoping Jason and Jonathan would show up.

Hans was all excited about his short time spent in the kitchen. Apparently, a fellow vegetable chopper was from the same region in Wales, where he was meeting his girlfriend the following weekend. He gave Hans the ins and outs of a few magical destinations only a local would know. It was priceless inside information for any world traveler.

Hans was beside himself and squealed to Jason, "Pretty lucky, ja?"

Jason looked at Hans, raised his eyebrows and said, "I don't think luck has much to do with it around here." Hans nodded in eager agreement as both of them wondered how many more magical coincidences may be in store.

Within a few minutes, Jonathan popped his head through the entry way of the cafe. Jason and Hans enthusiastically flagged him down, hoping to hear another synchronistic story. However, as Jonathan maneuvered his way through the coffee shop crowd, Jason and Hans could see he wasn't alone.

"Hey guys," Jonathan beamed. "This is Andrea. She's from Germany too."

Jason could instantly see sparks flying all over the place between the two new lovebirds. Andrea had just finished her studies in Homeopathy in Edinburgh and, like so many others, stopped by Findhorn to see if all the stories were true.

As introductions and small talk circled the table, Jason remember he'd purchased tickets for the upcoming workshop on Saturday. He asked Andrea if she wanted to go also but she had to return to Germany on the day of the event.

"I guess it's just you and me for the workshop, Johnny-boy," Jason sarcastically reminded Jonathan.

"Got it," Jonathan replied.

"Make sure to be there. That will be my last night here and you have the car."

An hour later, the coffee shop was just starting to thin out. Jason was feeling pangs of good ol' American guilt and figured it was time for him to get back to work. As the foursome dispersed to resume their duties, Jason looked Jonathan straight in the eye and said, "Don't get distracted. Workshop. Saturday. Be there."

"Yeah, yeah." Jonathan defended.

After tea, everyone vanished back to their work areas. Jason was confident his suspicions about Jonathan would soon be confirmed. They were. He didn't see Jonathan again until the workshop on Saturday. So much for all the excitement about finding the meaning behind Jason's visions.

*

In addition to cementing his new friendship with Hans, Jason spent the next week getting to know Ula, almost like a younger brother. She was fascinated to learn of his visions and adventures in Alaska.

When the conversation turned to her, Jason learned she was 15 years his senior and a direct descendent of Dutch royalty. She spent 12 years as a commodities trader in London where she amassed a fortune, on top of what she was born into. She had also married a very successful, high-rolling entrepreneur. They lived a child-free, face-paced, high-stress lifestyle—completely self-absorbed. Then, during a 36-hour, high society, partying binge on the Mediterranean, her closest girlfriend from college died of a drug overdose. About two weeks later, she caught her husband in bed with a younger woman.

Her life completely unraveled.

Shortly after, she came to Findhorn. It was her attempt to heal. She needed to reassess her priorities, pull herself back together, and chart a new course. That was about two years before she met Jason. As far as Jason could see, she seemed to be doing just fine.

Ula also indicated there was a small band of others like her at Findhorn. Jason then realized why work wasn't the number one priority at Findhorn. Through the generosity of its devoted members, Findhorn had access to millions.

*

Jason spent the week working in the gardens, taking hikes along Scotland's northern coast, and meeting as many new people as he could. It was a fascinating consortium of folks, from all over the northern hemisphere. There was every background and story imaginable. Some had stories and insights from mystical worlds that blew Jason away. However, no one was able to give him deeper insights into his visions from Chevron Mountain. Everyone had an opinion but nothing he could really hang his hat on.

Despite his disappointment, there was one visionary seer Ula directed Jason to meet. He was wise beyond the millennium and gave Jason the impression he knew the mysteries behind his visions. When Jason tired to probe him further, the old man just grinned and said, "You are most certainly on the right track, young man. Why do you want me to spoil all the surprise? You'll find out soon enough. However, you're being here is certainly no mistake. Oh…and don't forget your new friends."

Jason never forgot that comment.

Guide - The Octahedron

Saturday rolled around all too soon. About an hour before the workshop was to begin, the door to the caravan flung open and Jonathan strolled in, wearing an ear-to-ear grin.

"How was your time with Andrea?" Jason inquired.

"Great!" Jonathan shot back enthusiastically.

"You gonna see her again?" Jason pried.

"Nah," Jonathan shrugged nonchalantly. "She had to get back to her fiancé."

Jason glared in disgust and sneered. Then he changed the subject. "You ready for the workshop?"

"Damn straight! Let's go!"

So, off the two comrades went, thinking a gentle meditation would be the flawless ending to their near-perfect week. As they wandered over to the workshop studio, they openly wondered why a meditation event would take so long. All day for a meditation? They'd both been to meditation classes in the past. They couldn't imagine how one could take all day.

When they arrived at the studio, they were greeted by the Swiss facilitator, named Franz. He was a lean, 40-something, hippy-esque, free spirit with shoulder length, wavy, gray hair. Well prepared and clearly excited, he gave off the impression he'd been waiting for months to give this event.

Jason quickly learned, in part, why the event was going to last all day. The first hour alone was dedicated to introducing the unique meditation, called Holotropic Breathwork. Franz spent quiet some time discussing procedures, logistics and, quite honestly, what they were in for. The rules of the meditation were as follows:

First off, everyone was required to pair up with someone they didn't know. Second, the meditation was going to be split into two equal parts. At halftime, partners were to trade roles, switching meditator and assistant. The person meditating was allowed a small amount of water but no food before beginning. That was because too many past participants had puked their guts out.

When Jonathan heard that, he gave a panicked look to Jason across the room that said, "What the hell have we gotten ourselves into?"

Jason shrugged his shoulders and tilted his head back at Jonathan as if to say, "You wanted an adventure didn't you?"

When they later crossed paths in the bathroom during a break, Jason casually stated, "Well, this shouldn't be boring."

*

Because everyone would have their individualized experience, it was impossible to determine what would happen. However, history indicated a few possible scenarios. Those included, going out-of-body, releasing demons and entities, purging suppressed emotion, kundalini experiences, energy infusions, spiritual awakenings, Divine downloads and states of nirvana.

During the meditation, each participant was to lie on the floor with their assistant at their side. Then, they were to engage in non-stop, deep breathing until the end of their meditation. The deep breathing induced a state of hyperventilation which caused the physical body to painfully cramp up. That supposedly opened the subconscious mind. An assistant was needed to make sure the deep breathing didn't stop and to provide reassurance, in case of excessive trauma.

Jason teamed up with a naturopathic doctor from Dublin, named Derek. He looked a bit like a madman in the throes of a midlife crisis. He said he'd done a couple of similar workshops before and that they were nothing short of amazing. Apparently, Breathwork helped Dr. Jekyll discover his inner Mr. Hyde.

Because he was a newbie, Jason got to go first. Apprehensively, he laid down on his mat on the carpeted studio floor. As he closed his eyes and started to breathe, Franz switched off the lights and turned the music on. It was loud, driving, intense African drumming. The music alone almost launched Jason into another dimension.

With encouragement from Derek, Jason began to belly breathe for the longest time, yet nothing seemed to happen. However, in the darkness of the studio, he could hear people flopping around and wailing through the deafening music. He also felt the ground thunder, as if a herd of wild animals stampeded through the studio. After that, he felt a warm tropical breeze, scented with the potent aroma of Patchouli. Something was certainly happening, he just didn't know what.

Jason became increasingly uncomfortable with the breathing. Frustrated and annoyed, he was about to quit and go back to the caravan. But Derek was right there, encouraging him to stick with it. "Almost there," he whispered in support. Jason disagreed strongly and decided it was time to pack it in. This bunk simply wasn't for him. As he lurched in an attempt to get up, he realized his body was stiff. He couldn't sit upright. His hands were cramped, bent at a bizarre angle, and he couldn't move his legs. Then he started to panic. Nevertheless, the voice of Derek hovered above in the darkness. "Keep breathing. That's it. You're doing great. Keep breathing." Derek's soothing voice was the last thing Jason remembered about being in the studio.

Instantly, Jason exploded into a colorful but dimly lit tunnel or wormhole, traveling at what seemed like the speed of sound. He was horrified, as his eyelids peeled back from a monstrous g-force.

Rocketing forward, he thought he heard screaming in the distance. Or maybe it was his voice; he wasn't sure. Continuing to accelerate, he whizzed by a blur of images and events. Were they from his childhood? Past lives, maybe? He couldn't tell. His attention was glued forward. It was everything he could do to keep from crumbling into hysterics, as he continued to gain momentum.

When he reached the end of the tunnel, he was blasted into a completely different environment, like a cliff diver piercing an emerald sea below. Abruptly, he was slowed to a crawl, floating and suspended in space. In the distance, he could see points of light. "Stars? Galaxies? Solar Systems?" he wondered, as he drifted into a state of deep stillness.

Slowly, he drifted toward the points of light. However, in the blackness of space, he had no depth perception. He couldn't tell if the illuminations were light years away or just beyond his grasp. Time, space and perception had all been seriously distorted.

As the lights drew near, he saw an entire squadron of geometric images, very similar to those on Chevron Mountain. Countless images floated by in the weightlessness of space. Caught up in the spectacle of the moment, Jason didn't give a thought to their meaning. However, a flash of the Inuit Elder passed through his brain and he realized this was his first encounter with the guides he was commissioned to seek out.

In the distance, he saw the brightest star coming directly at him. It reminded him of the Great Star in the East, associated with the birth of Jesus. As it slowly approached, radiating incredible light, Jason saw it was the golden octahedron from Chevron Mountain. Soon, it hovered about a familiar arm's length away. As Jason stared on, it accelerated at warp speed, entered his body, and detonated into his heart. The reverberating shockwave ripped through Jason's layers of consciousness, like an explosion. He gasped a violent exhalation of breath, then coughed, like someone who'd nearly drowned. And just like that, Jason was awake, back in the darkened studio.

Groggy and traumatized, Jason propped himself up with his arms. Derek was right there, offering comfort and support. "How you doin?" he asked.

"Fine, fine," Jason thought he heard himself say. "How long was I gone?"

"About three hours." Derek replied.

"Three hours?!?! It felt like ten minutes!"

As Jason strained to regain consciousness, he looked down and noticed he'd wet his pants.

"Don't worry about that," Derek consoled. "That kind of stuff happens all the time. We'll clean it up. Plus, I'm next. I can get real messy."

Jason snuck a peek over at Jonathan, who looked severely disturbed and very pale. He had also broken his glasses. So much for a gentle meditation to cap off the near-perfect week.

Jason was in such a sorry state after his meditation, he didn't think he'd be any help at all for Derek. Lucky for Jason, Derek had plenty of experience in breathwork and walked himself through the experience solo. About 10 minutes after the workshop had finished, Jason couldn't even remember what Derek went through, other than a vague memory of violent scratching and blood curdling howls.

Triangle One
When all was said and done, Jason and Jonathan slowly made their way back to the caravan in the dark. Jonathan had to stop a few times to dry heave in the bushes. His breathwork experience had led straight to his father. Apparently, the two of them battled for hours on end with medieval weapons. Jonathan eventually ended up the victor by splatting his dad's head with a spiked ball on the end of a chain. It seemed fitting because Jonathan had a

few deep-seated father issues, mainly because he'd never met his dad. The bastard (Jonathan's words) skipped out on his Mom, soon after he got her pregnant. Because his Dad wasn't around, Jonathan had to settle his differences with his dad in the nether world.

Jason arrived at the caravan first because Jonathan was still fertilizing the bushes. As he reached for the door handle in the dark, his foot struck something that made a small clanking sound. Inquisitively fumbling around on his hands and knees, he felt a piece of cold metal with his fingertips. Jason stood up, just as a very pale Jonathan arrived. "Whatcha got there?" he asked.

Curiously holding it up to the light, Jason replied, "I dunno. Looks like somebody dropped some jewelry." Jonathan glanced at the metal object in Jason's hand and stumbled into the caravan. He grabbed the closest bottle of water he could find, took a huge swig, and promptly crashed into bed.

Jason flicked on the table light and began to study his new found trinket. It was a yellow, metallic, equilateral triangle, about three inches long on each side. Nearly one-eighth inch thick, it was pretty heavy for its size. At first glance, he thought it was some type of gold. So he pulled a coin out of his pocket and gave it a scratch. His jaw dropped. Yellow metal rubbed off on the coin. It was gold! And as far as he could figure, it was very pure. His hand immediately started shaking and his mind went crazy.

The edges were beveled and two of the three sides had small tabs, extending from the midpoint. The third side, which seemed like the bottom, had a small indentation in the middle. The tabs and indentation gave the triangle the semblance of a piece to a jigsaw puzzle. On what appeared to be the front face, was a symbol in the center. Above and below that symbol were lines of text. The text was from an alphabet Jason didn't recognize.

The back of the triangle was completely filled with symbols. Jason had been exposed to systems of ancient divination, such as, Astrology and the Runes, and recognized a few from there. However, he couldn't tell if a message read left to right, right to left, top to bottom, or bottom to top. Maybe, he thought, a message was relayed through the groupings of certain symbols. Or maybe, each symbol stood on its own like elements in the periodic table of chemistry. Of course, he had no clue as to what any of it meant. However, he was pretty sure of one thing: The triangle was not from this world. It was old, ancient.

Jason couldn't get his mind to slow down. He'd literally stumbled onto a priceless heirloom. "But how did it get there? Whose is it?" Then his mind latched on to the memory of the golden octahedron from his breathwork meditation and the visions from Chevron Mountain. "Could it be? Is this a piece to the octahedron?" It was more than his weary mind could fathom. For sanity's sake, he needed to temporarily let it go and give it a rest for the night.

Jason wrapped the triangle in paper towels, slipped it into a sandwich bag and tucked it into the lapel pocket inside his rain coat. Then, he hopped into the shower until the hot water ran out, crawled into bed, and crashed into a dreamless night's sleep.

The next morning Jason didn't know what to do. He wasn't even sure if he should say anything to Jonathan. But he knew there was no way he could keep it to himself. At least by sharing his find with Jonathan, they could bounce some ideas around on what to do next.

When Jonathan finally dragged himself out of bed, he headed straight for the coffee pot. "Some workshop yesterday, huh?" he said. "I had nightmares all night long. How 'bout you?"

"I was pretty restless," Jason replied, "But I eventually caught a few winks. Remember this?" he said, as he held the triangle in the air.
"Oh yeah," Jonathan said, mildly surprised, as he poured some coffee. "I almost forgot about that. Mind if I give it a look?"

Jason carefully placed it on the table, with a cloth underneath to protect its surface. Jonathan look closely but didn't touch. "Sheee-it," Jonathan blurted in amazement. "Where did you find it?"

"I stumbled over it when I opened the caravan door last night," Jason replied, as he gently flipped it over.

"Do you think someone lost it?"

"No clue," Jason responded. "What do you think I should do?"

"Pawn it," Jonathan sarcastically sniped. "You could get a small fortune of beer money for the rest of the trip and then some."

Jason laughed then responsibly thought out loud, "I think I should notify the office, in case someone lost it. If they can describe it, I'll give it back. I'll leave my contact info with whoever's in charge of lost and found."

Jonathan nodded in ethical agreement and with a three-fingered salute spouted, "Very boy scout of you."

Before heading over to the office, Jason painstakingly copied the etchings from the triangle onto a piece of paper. He hoped someone at Findhorn might know something. Then, he quickly jogged over to the office to report his finding of lost jewelry. When he finished, he pulled the copy of the etchings out of his pocket and asked the administrator if she knew anyone who might be able to decipher the language.

According to her, one of the co-founders of the Findhorn Foundation was a former linguistics professor. His office was in the next building over. Jason immediately set out and after asking around, finally tracked him down in the art studio. He was a polite and enthusiastic old chap. He entertained Jason's request immediately and studied the meticulously written language on the paper. Without thinking twice, he stated in a British accent, "It's probably

Arabic, most likely from ancient Egypt. I'm afraid I'm a little rusty, so I can't translate the message. If it's really important to you, contact Dr. Seymour Hedgewick at Cambridge University. He's one of the best at this sort of thing." Jason eagerly gave thanks and darted back to the caravan to tell Jonathan.

That day was to be Jason's and Jonathan's last day in Findhorn. However, they still had a few days before catching their return flight at Heathrow. So to finish off the trip, they planned to spend the last couple of days in Edinburgh. On the drive there, Jason filled Jonathan in on Dr. Hedgewick and Cambridge. Jason desperately wanted to extend their travels for few more days to visit the University.

"Can't do it," Jonathan said. "I called home while you were running around this morning. I got an offer on my house."

Before leaving for Findhorn, both Jason and Jonathan suspected it might be a life-changing adventure. Jonathan had put his house on the market shortly before they left. They both knew their days as roommates were numbered. The adventure to Findhorn marked the end of an era.

Solemnly, Jason said, "Guess, I'll have to go solo."

"Guess so," Jonathan agreed.

Breathwork Fallout
By early afternoon, our heroes made it to their hostel-style hotel, near the center of Edinburgh. After cramming themselves into their room, which was a smidge larger than a clothes closet, they made plans for their last couple of days in the Scottish capital. "There's no better place to sip Scotch whiskey than in Scotland," Jonathan said, with a mischievous look on his face. Apparently, his stomach had recovered from the workshop.

Jason balked hard and responded, "C'mon. Franz gave us specific instructions to abstain from drugs and alcohol for at least a week after the workshop. We both know dark energies may have been released that can possibly exit through the events of our lives. My body is still trying to assimilate whatever the hell happened back at the workshop. My guts are churning something ugly."

Jonathan shook his head in disbelief, annoyed Jason would let an epic Scottish adventure pass him by. "Franz-schmanz,"Jonathan teased. "What are you going to do, stay locked up in this stamp-sized room all night? C'mon. Let's go, before it gets dark." With that gentle arm-twisting, Jason submitted. In a matter of minutes, they were outside, cruising the ancient streets of Edinburgh.

They wandered the streets for an hour or more, before landing in a downstairs pub, fashioned in the theme of a medieval dungeon. Jonathan promptly ordered a straight shot of Scotland's finest. Jason, on the other hand, ordered a Guinness Stout, a sacrilegious foul to the highest degree, according to Jonathan. "Irish beer in Scotland. Disgraceful," he joked, raising his glass in cheers.

An hour, some reminiscing, and a few of drinks later, the boys floated back up to street level just as the sun was going down. "Which way back?" Jonathan asked with a moderate buzz.

Jason shrugged and said, "Beats me. But there's no way in hell, I'm pulling my map out in this shady neighborhood. We'll be targeted as tourists for sure. You might as well paint a bull's eye on our backs."

So the two of them uncomfortably strolled away from the pub. Daylight was fading and overhead lights were twitching to life. The historic alleyways that seemed delightful only minutes ago, took on a disturbingly unfriendly aura as the gloom of darkness slowly descended. The personality of the neighborhood completely transformed, like a werewolf on a full moon. Empty street corners by day were now claimed by seedy loiterers. Jason guessed they were drug dealers and who-knows-what-else. With each progressive step, uneasiness settled on the young American tourists, who were quickly realizing they had landed on the wrong side of the Scottish tracks.

It didn't matter which way they walked, every street seemed dangerous. Furthermore, they couldn't get their bearings in the maze of twisted streets. Each new street seemed darker than the last, and their collective, alcohol-fueled, anxiety was exponentially starting to climb.

Suddenly in the darkness, they were approached from behind. It was a thin, wiry, longhaired man somewhere in his 30s wearing a full-length, tattered street coat. "Spare change?" he aggressively inquired through his yellowed, broken teeth. Jason and Jonathan quickly exchanged a panicked glance. This guy had an American accent...and was living on Scottish streets. They were pegged.

"No, sorry man," Jason replied, as both he and Jonathan hurried their step to leave him behind. A few seconds later, he bolted up from behind and stood squarely in front of them, stopping them in their tracks.

"Don't shine me on, man!" he screamed at the top of his lungs, with crazed eyes of a schizophrenic junkie. Then, he flashed an enormous knife, hidden under his coat. Jonathan gasped and emptied his pockets as quickly as he could, gifting the junked-out thief a tidy sum of about ten pounds in coin. Instantly, the American pirate absconded with the treasure and dashed off into the nearest alley to purchase his next fix.

The young American tourists were now horrified, as well as lost. They quickened their pace to a slow run. Each loitering drug dealer gave a wide berth to the boys as they passed. They knew victims freshly hit were an unpredictable commodity, indeed.

They pressed on aimlessly for the next several hours, in a moderated drunken state of panic, in a city they did not know. When all seemed lost, Jason finally stopped in helpless fatigue and looked skyward, praying for help. That's when the guiding hand of their guardian angel appeared. Miraculously, they were standing under the sign of their hotel.

Breathing a huge sigh of relief, they trudged up to their room. Apparently, the horror of the night's events and the fine Scotch whiskey didn't settle too well with Jonathan's system. He went back to fertilizing the bushes again, this time in the toilet down the hall. As Jason listened to the wrenching of Jonathan in the distance, he wished they would have listened and adhered to the instructions of Franz.

Cambridge

Jonathan awoke early the next morning and promptly announced that his European vacation was over. He couldn't wait to get the hell out of Scotland. He agreed to drop Jason off in Cambridge and then head directly to Heathrow, a day early. He was glad to spend the night in the airport, just as long as it wasn't Scotland. Jason, on the other hand, planned to stay on in England and get answers on the triangle, or until his money ran out.

About six hours later, they were in Cambridge, England. When Jonathan pulled the car in front of Jason's hostel, the two of them sat in the awkward silence of finality, for quite some time. Eventually, Jason mustered his courage, opened the door and walked back to the boot. With a small sigh, he pulled out his bag. Jonathan slowly followed suit, looking at the ground the entire time.

"Well, I guess this is it," Jason said with a pang of sincere endearment. Jonathan looked up as if about to weep. He didn't say a word, as the two best of friends embraced in an enormous heartfelt goodbye.

"I should only be a few days, if that," Jason said.

"Take your time," Jonathan replied. "I'll see you when you get back. Good luck."

With another brief man-hug, the two buddies parted. Jonathan drove off to find the motorway. Jason turned toward the lobby, deliberately attending to the business of high adventure.

When Jason checked into the hostel, he noticed the rooms weren't designated by number or name. They were labeled with geometric shapes. His room, ironically enough, was the Triangle room. Gently laughing to himself, he remembered the Inuit Elder said he would be guided with many signs along the way. As he opened the door to his tiny suite, he felt as if his geometric guardian angel was right by his side.

Dr. Seymour Hedgewick
Jason didn't waste any time. He dropped off his bag and headed straight to the university to find Dr. Hedgewick. After asking a few people for directions, he finally ended up at the Department of Archeology and went directly into the office. The secretary politely informed him that Dr. Hedgewick was in London for the remainder of the day. However, he would return the following day to resume his normal schedule. She also informed him that he didn't need an appointment. Dr. Hedgewick had open office hours from 4:00 to 5:00 each day. Jason could just drop in. With a nod of gratitude, Jason excused himself and spent the rest of the day absorbed in the history of Cambridge.

At 4:00 the next afternoon, Jason was knocking on the half-opened door of Dr. Seymour Hedgewick. No one was there. With a sense of curiosity that overshadowed his guilt, he pushed the door open and stepped in. The place was a mess. There were journals, periodicals and papers in various piles. Some reached over half way to the ceiling. There were overstuffed filing cabinets that could no longer close. One wall was adorned with a multitude of photographs. Stapled from the floor to the ceiling, were countless artifacts, archeological digs, temples, treasures of all sorts, and a few mug shots of a beaming explorer in exotic and far-away lands.

"Hmmm...," Jason muttered to himself. "That must be Hedgewick."

However, the most interesting were the artifacts scattered throughout the office. There was a tarnished, ornately designed golden candlestick propped on top of a filing cabinet. There were a variety of ancient-looking bowls, tools and masks, strewn on the floor along one wall. But the creepiest memento was the pair of human skulls on the far corner table, lying on what looked like a pile of sample bags.

Suddenly, Jason was snapped out of his office inspection by a very curt and defiant announcement of arrival. "Excuse me, sir! May I help you?" It was the very Dr. Seymour Hedgewick.

Embarrassed, Jason quickly introduced himself and the purpose of his visit. As the two exchanged guarded pleasantries, Jason carefully sized-up Dr. Hedgewick. He was in his late 30s, modestly good looking, intelligent, brash, overly self-confident, slightly pompous, a tad arrogant, charismatic, humorous, positive, energetic and infectiously charming. Jason liked him immediately. Furthermore, it wasn't a stretch to imagine Dr. Hedgewick roaming in distant catacombs wearing an explorer's outfit and a pith helmet.

Hedgewick quickly positioned himself behind his cluttered desk, plopped in his squeaky chair and inquired, "So, you have an artifact, do you?" Immediately, his arm shot forward, palm up. He motioned with his fingers, as if to say, "Okay, hand it over. Give us a look." Then he rolled his eyes in mild annoyance as if he were thinking, "Not another one. This should take about two seconds."

Jason carefully reached into his lapel pocket and pulled out the triangle, wrapped in paper towels and plastic. Hedgewick cleared a spot on his desk and pulled out a padded tray, as if to humor Jason. Instead of handing the triangle to Hedgewick, Jason carefully placed it on the tray.

Hedgewick didn't immediately reply with his usual canned response of, "Sorry…it's a fake. Thanks for stopping by. Don't forget to visit our lovely teahouse down by the rose gardens." Instead, what followed was about three minutes of a very uncomfortable, edge-of-your-seat silence. Time was completely suspended.

Hedgewick gave Jason a few serious and inquisitive glances, then reached into his drawer and pulled out a pair of latex gloves. He snapped the gloves on like a surgeon, pulled out a pair of high-octane glasses, and scrutinized the triangle thoroughly. Peering at Jason for permission to touch the triangle, Hedgewick inquired, "May I?" Jason nodded and Hedgewick delicately turned the artifact over. Without wasting another thought, Hedgewick snapped up his phone and placed a quick call.

"Higgins, old boy, Hedgewick here. Would you be so kind and pop over to my office? There's something you need to see."

"Dr. Higgins," Hedgewick explained with a sarcastic grin, "is an expert in ancient linguistics...languages, alphabets and so-forth. I'm just an archeologist. I dig around in ancient graveyards, garbage dumps and latrines looking for jewelry, tools, pots and pans, and what-not."

Within minutes, Dr. Higgins arrived, carrying the presence of a standard British scholar: serious, soft around the edges, spectacles and a fine tweed suit. For the next 15 minutes, Higgins and Hedgewick studied the triangle in silence. They exchanged a few odd glances, but mostly, their minds were whirling at about a million miles per hour. Jason watched on in helpless anticipation.

Hedgewick finally looked up at Jason and asked, "Mr. Sananda, would you be so kind as to leave this specimen with us for a few days? We'd like to study it further."

Jason had been through the halls of higher academia and knew how prized artifacts could mysteriously go missing; especially when placed in the hands of greedy professors. Plus, the state of

Hedgewick's office was lousy PR for anyone wanting a treasured possession to be kept safe and sound.

In defiance, Jason firmly straightened himself up. With daggers in his eyes, he replied with total conviction, "No way."

Hedgewick awkwardly cleared his throat and was taken aback, as if he were caught with his hand in the cookie jar. Quickly grasping at straws in attempt to make a recovery, he said, "How about letting us snap a few photos then? What say…tomorrow about this time?"

Jason, feeling a surge of momentary power, snapped back, "What's in it for me? And please don't say 'For the Betterment of Science'."

Hedgewick thought for a moment and said, "Tell you what. You let us photograph your artifact and I'll send you a report on our findings."

Jason kicked it around in his head for a moment then cautiously replied, "Okay. See you tomorrow at 4:00."

As Jason packed away the triangle, he noticed how the previous 30 minutes had perked up the spirits of the two professors. They were almost giddy. Jason wasn't exactly sure what happened. However, he was passionately informed, he was now on a first name basis with Seymour.

Jason arrived promptly at 4:00 the next day. Only this time, he was eagerly greeted by Seymour, Higgins and a lab tech named Simon. They immediately led him down the hallway and into the basement. On the walk to the lower level, Jason assumed the photo shoot would probably take about a half hour. He was hoping that would give him plenty of time to catch an interesting lecture on astronomy that was being held on campus at 7:00. With that thought rumbling in his head, they reached an ordinary door with a metal nameplate that simply read "Lab."

When the door creaked open and the light flicked on, Jason couldn't believe his eyes. It was an enormous warehouse filled with artifacts and treasures from all over the world. The storeroom smelled musty and dank but everything was neatly labeled, numbered, organized and categorized, nothing like Seymour's office. As Jason stepped in and began to browse around, he realized he was in very privileged company. He also understood, he was in a place very few people would ever get to see. The Smithsonian would have been very jealous.

Seymour proudly waved his hand and said, "This way." Following his lead, they paraded through a maze of ceiling-high shelves, cabinets and drawers until they reached an unmarked door. Seymour stopped in front of the door. Wielding a guilty grin, he pumped his eye brows a few times, reached in his pocket for a key, and unlocked the door. He flung the door open and proclaimed, "Behold! Welcome to my Empire!" It was a state-of-the-art photography studio with every picture taking gadget known to mankind. Seymour winked at Jason and wryly admitted, "Sizable grant money, from well-established institutions, has a way of funding elaborate hobbies for certain lucky researchers!" Apparently, besides archeology, Seymour had a passion for photography.

What Jason assumed was going to be a 30-minute photo session with a cheap Polaroid, turned into a six-hour, high-tech affair. So much for the astronomy lecture.

Throughout the evening, Seymour, Higgins and Simon worked meticulously and took photos from every angle, resolution, magnification and lighting arrangement imaginable. They certainly left Jason with the impression they were very interested in the artifact.

Between photographs, Jason wandered around the warehouse and viewed treasures that would have turned any museum aficionado green with envy. The specimen that caught his attention most was a bear fetus in a jar of formaldehyde. Another sign. "I guess I'm on the right path," he thought. However, bear fetus aside, this was like most other visits he'd had to museums. It didn't take him too long to get bored. So he drifted back into the photo session and asked Seymour a few questions, one in particular.

"Do you think the triangle is solid gold?"

"Highly unlikely," Seymour said, intently focused on setting up his next shot. "My guess is that the triangle was crafted in or around Egypt, sometime around the era of King Tut. I won't know for certain until I have a chance to study the highly magnified photos is detail. The odd thing is…well…it's the language, the blasted alphabet and symbols. That's where Higgins comes in. He knows way more about such things than I do. But at first look, it doesn't seem to add up. Neither Higgins nor I have seen anything like it before."

When the last photo was taken, Jason could see Seymour wasn't a man who went home tired at the end of the day. He went home energized because he loved what he did. That night in particular, his enthusiasm was especially inspirational. Everyone finished the project deeply satisfied, feeling like they had accomplished something very important.

When everything was neatly packed up, the team quietly shuffled out the door. After Seymour locked the door, he turned around and joked to Jason, "Better not forget this." He was waving the wrapped triangle in his hand.

"Oh, yeah…that," Jason blushed, then sheepishly reached out with his hand. Forgetting the triangle in Seymour's photo lab would have been a real boo-boo. That was a scenario he had no intention of playing out in his head.

Jason, Seymour, Higgins and Simon trekked back to Seymour's office and parted as what Jason loosely thought of as friends. He had enjoyed their company immensely. As they shook hands and said their farewells, Seymour chirped in, "I'm going to get on this right away and send you a report as soon as I'm able. You haven't seen the last of Dr. Seymour Hedgewick yet!" As Jason turned and exited into the night, he had the feeling Dr. Seymour may be very well be right.

The Report
Jason was worn out from the events of the previous week. More than anything, he wanted to stop and assimilate it all. He had no desire to head straight back home. Unfortunately, his allotment of stockpiled funds were drying up fast. So he decided to fly back to New York and take a leisurely three-day bus trip across the heart of his homeland. The only comment he had as he stepped out, hunched over in Seattle was, "Boy, that was a bad idea." However, the bus trip gave him time to recommit to his mission, hoping Seymour's findings would provide some additional insight.

When Jason made it back to Jonathan's house, nothing was the same. The house had been sold and he had two weeks to move out. The place was in a disarray of upended rooms and half-packed boxes. However, Jason's room was untouched, except for a stack of unopened mail. There was no word from Findhorn or anyone wanting to reclaim lost jewelry.

Jason was a minimalist, so moving his stuff out was no big deal. He simply rented a cheap storage unit and reluctantly asked his widowed mother if he could crash in her basement for a while. She was delighted. Jason, on the other hand, was pretty embarrassed. He just hoped none of the neighbors would notice and thanked God dear ol' Mom was a master at giving him his space.

When moving day arrived, there were no tears. All the necessary good-byes had been said in England. This was a hopeful day of new beginnings; Jonathan's new ship was christened and ready to set sail. When the last box was loaded into the truck, Jonathan asked, "One more coffee for old time's sake? I'm buyin'." Jason nodded with delight and within minutes, the two old pals were settled in for their last cup of Joe together. As soon as they sat down, Jonathan reached into his daypack and said, "I've got something for you." Then he pulled out a large white envelope and slapped in down on the table.

Jason recognized it immediately. It was an express international mailer with Seymour's handwriting on it. "Looks like your report's here," Jonathan said. "Quite honestly, I'm surprised it came at all. C'mon open it up."

Jason wasn't so sure he wanted to. He knew there was a possibility his hopes, dreams and visions could collapse into a heap on the floor. Hesitantly, he grabbed a butter knife and used it as a letter opener.

Jason's immediate response when he pulled the report out was, "Wow." It was at least twenty pages of in-depth analytical assessment, with another dozen or more color photographs attached. "I can't read this now," Jason complained, like a college kid who just had and enormous assignment laid on him. "I'll have to let you know what it says later. This could take a few days."

"What's that on top?" Jonathan inquired, craning his neck.

"Looks like a cover letter and a news clipping."

The letter was from Seymour, very polite and professional, briefly explaining the contents. There was also some strongly worded encouragement, to please stay in touch and keep him abreast of developments. The news article was a recent item from the London Times. The headline read, "Cambridge Professor Discovers Ancient Egyptian Artifact." It was followed by several paragraphs with Seymour's name plastered all over it. Of course, there was no mention of Dr. Higgins or Jason. At the bottom of the article was a photograph of the triangle.

When Jason saw the photo, he gasped and his eyes nearly popped out of his head. All he managed to utter was a very shaky, "Oh, no." Suddenly, he felt very vulnerable, almost violated.

Jonathan grinned and sarcastically sneered, "Looks like your pal Dr. Seymour is trying to make himself famous with your triangle. Lucky for me, I'm moving a couple hundred miles away. But it sure looks like the fun and games are just starting for you."

After downing a couple of strong Americanos and discussing the report at length, our heroes drove back to Jonathan's former home. Without much ado, they parted into the destiny of their new lives. Jonathan was headed a few hours south. Jason went home to have dinner with his Mommy.

After supper that night, Jason locked himself into his basement bedroom and anxiously pulled out Seymour's report. For added effect, he made a small alter opposite his bed and propped the triangle up on display. The report was divided into three primary sections: 1) Date of Fabrication, 2) Text and 3) Symbols.

Date of Fabrication
Seymour's suspicions about the date of the triangle were nowhere close to what he later found to be accurate. He concluded with 95 percent confidence, the triangle was fabricated as early as 2500 B.C., in ancient Egypt. During that time, gold was crafted through a crude technique referred to as a sheathing. The text and symbols were most likely carved into some type of hardwood first. Then, thin sheets of gold were pounded and pressed into place, resulting in a somewhat coarse texture. Sheathing eventually died out as more sophisticated gilding techniques evolved. To accentuate his findings, Seymour sent a number of magnified photographs, highlighting his theory of varying gold textures.

"Man, oh man," Jason thought. "If the triangle is a preserved gold and hardwood artifact, over 4,000 years old, it's worth a fortune."

The Text
Deciphering the text on the front of the triangle wasn't so straight forward because there were only a few lines. It was a small sample size. However, a few things were very clear.

First, the text was written in style of Akkadian cuneiform, the writing system of ancient Mesopotamia. It was an etched symbology, usually scribed into clay, prevalent in the day of King Tut (1500 - 1000 B.C.). Prime examples were the clay tablets, called the Amarna Letters, discovered by local Egyptian explorers in the late 1800's. The twenty-four tablet set were diplomatic correspondences between ancient Egyptian administrations. According to Seymour, the text glyphs on the triangle and the Amarna Letters were nearly identical. He included more comparison photos.

Second, was the content and syntax of the language. Unlike the Amarna letters, the content of the text was not political but spiritual. Furthermore, as far as Seymour could tell, there may have been a link between the message on the front of the triangle and an ancient spiritual text, called The Emerald Tablets. The Emerald Tablets were from the Hermetic tradition, written in Arabic somewhere between 500 and 800 A.D. They were highly influential in spiritual circles throughout Egypt and Europe, being translated into many different languages.

Seymour noticed the sentence structure and the language on the triangle was strikingly similar to The Emerald Tablets. In fact, he surmised, part of the text may have been a direct quote. To interpret the text more completely, Seymour turned to Dr. Higgins for help. Together, they were able to roughly translate the message on the front of the triangle into modern English:

"It is Truth, no lie, certain, and to be depended upon. Human anguish cannot be avoided. Like a serpent chasing its tail, it repeats from within. Learn this and know the soul."

The Symbols
The single symbol on the front of the triangle, between lines of text, was an Ouroboros, an ancient circular symbol, depicting a serpent eating its own tail. It had historically been associated with cyclicality, especially in the sense of something constantly re-creating itself. The first known Ouroboros was found in the tomb of

King Tut. Like the text, it was probably carved in hardwood, then sheathed with gold.

On the back, there were twenty-one symbols, all roughly the same size. They were aligned in a formation similar to bowling pins, forming a triangle inside the triangle. Seymour's findings quickly pointed out, the symbols were not confined to Egyptian culture. Most came from other civilizations, schools of thought, and belief systems spanning a vast consortium of time and space. Some of the symbols, Seymour didn't recognize at all.

The peculiarity of the symbols clearly came to light, when photographed under high magnification. Without question, it was clear the images were not carvings or etchings in wood, as one would expect from an artifact fabricated by sheathing. They were three-dimensional iconic figurines, intricately embedded into the triangle. Seymour also included two high-magnification photos of the symbols that were identical. The only difference was they were taken thirty minutes apart. It was unmistakable. All of the symbols had rotated to varying degrees in half an hour. The symbols were constantly in motion.

At the end of his report, Seymour didn't offer any formal conclusions. However, he did include an unofficial communiqué on a separate piece of paper. It was titled "Personal Side Notes—For Mr. Jason C. Sananda Only." It read as follows:

Dear Jason,

Thank you once again for sharing your most spectacular find with me. I am truly honored. I hope you realize from the enclosed report, the artifact you have stumbled upon is quite rare indeed.

As you know, I am man of empirical science. I stand on collected evidence, thorough analytic observations and research, and do my utmost to arrive at impartial conclusions. I have seen and handled many bona fide ancient artifacts, as well as many fraudulent counterfeits. After meeting you and handling the specimen personally, I have no doubt of its genuine authenticity. However, after additional research and detailed review of the photographs, I'm inclined to stray away from the scientific method. The facts just don't add up.

With that said, I believe all the factual information collected is accurate. The artifact was fabricated somewhere around 2500 B.C. The 'alphabet' used in writing the text is from roughly 1250 B.C. The style of the language, and possibly quoted material, is from about 650 A.D.

An analogy would be like this: Someone writes a message on a piece of Papyrus paper from the time and place of Arabic Jesus. However, it's written in the English alphabet of Shakespeare, quoting computer language from the 21st century. It just isn't possible; it doesn't make sense. That's because when the message was written, Shakespeare and computers hadn't yet come into existence.

Furthermore, the intricacy and complexity of the minute three-dimensional symbols on the back, rotating under their own power, is far beyond the technology that even exists today. I am not a man inclined to metaphysics. However, it may be possible that the symbols on the back of the triangle radiate encrypted information from higher intelligences; similar to crop circles, Stonehenge and the Great Pyramids themselves.

Therefore, my dear Mr. Sananda, my hunch (that I reveal to only you) is that your precious artifact may not have been crafted by human hands at all. However, if it was fabricated from someone within our genetic makeup, I seriously doubt they are from this time. With great caution I'm guessing, your relict may well be from another time, possibly the future. If this is true, then it's within the realm of feasibility, that your triangular treasure is an actual living creature.

Again, these are not formal conclusions, only personal speculations. Much more research would be needed to publish anything so utterly outside the mental compartmentalization of the scientific community. If you have any desire to have the triangle researched in more detail, please let me know. I'm confident funding options would be easily available.

Thank you again, and please, do stay in touch. If there is anything you ever need, please contact me at once.

Most Respectfully,
Seymour

P.S. If you have no objections, I'd like to publish my research and findings from the photographs I've taken of the triangle.

Jason was up the next morning at 7:00 a.m., placing a call to the venerated Dr. Seymour Hedgewick. His feelings of violation, anger and mistrust evaporated as soon as Jason heard his voice. Seymour was simply too charming. After exchanging hearty greetings, Jason thanked Seymour for the report. He also gave his consent for Seymour to publish any scientific papers regarding the triangle, under one condition. That condition was: That under no circumstance whatsoever, was Seymour to reveal Jason's name, location or any other personal information. Jason hated the idea of being in the public eye. Plus, he didn't want to get robbed. Seymour agreed immediately. He had no problem with hogging the spotlight.

*

The Search for Truth
For the next three years, Jason dedicated his life to what he thought the triangle was guiding him to do. That was searching for Truth. He dove head-first into traditional disciplines that seemed like obvious paths to that door, namely religion and psychology. It was a passionate attempt to discover deeper purpose and meaning in life. He assumed the route to the Truth was through rational thinking and conscious understanding.

Religion
Overnight, Jason became a fervent zealot. He devoured books from every faith and religious persuasion. He read the Bible, the Koran, the Torah, the Bhagavad Gita, and many other sacred historical texts. His mind soaked in religious philosophies and the-

ologies like a sponge. However, all the reading in the world couldn't satisfy the inner burning for a rational Truth. The problem was, he didn't exactly know what he was looking for.

Then, he decided to try something he'd never done before. He went to church. Or rather, churches…and synagogues…and mosques…and temples. He hunted down every organized religious community he could find. He met many wonderful and not so wonderful people. He picked their brains, dissected their experiences, and probed into their underlying belief in a God.

However, there were certain limitations to his search. First off, his part of the world was predominantly Christian. He wasn't sure if eyes focused on a strictly Christian God could encompass his universal pursuit of Truth. Furthermore, the more people he talked to, the more divisiveness he discovered. In fact, a few churches were nothing but systems of conformity and self-righteousness—judgmental and fervent promoters of mediocrity. That turned him off like a cold faucet.

Eventually, Jason placed his bet on the Catholic church and spent a year in the seminary, studying to become a priest. His decision was based on the longevity of the Catholic tradition and a solid, scholarly, academic theology. Jason thought it was the most intelligent understanding of a higher Truth. Just what his rational mind told him he was looking for.

However, after a year, Jason realized the Catholic church was not only scholarly but highly political. Furthermore, the dogma, rules and open discrimination were too much for his young, free-spirited and rebellious nature. He ended up not only leaving the Catholic church but all religions and faiths. He became deeply disillusioned. As disappointed as he was, he reminded himself that disillusionment was a good thing. Illusion couldn't serve his quest for the Truth.

In the end, Jason viewed religion as a mere construct of the human mind. Religion seemed like a rationally concocted system to entice people to believe in something. Something invented by someone else. In the beginning, that's what he thought wanted. However, as his belief in God evolved, it left him feeling empty. Then one day, the lights flashed on and he understood. He didn't want to believe in God. He wanted to experience God.

Psychology
During his quest for Truth through religion, Jason simultaneously had his spotlight focused inward. He was taking a long, hard look at his inner world. He was at the age when personal suffering starts to emerge and was in the throes of some very deep pain. So one night, he sat down and listed all of his problems. His list looked something like this.

Life Challenges
Family history of alcoholism
Problems with work and money
    - always afraid of bosses
    - internal conflict about jobs
    - never like what I do for money
    - unstable, I either get laid off, fired or I quit
Girlfriends
    - can't keep one, tend to get dumped
    - lousy boundaries

To put it mildly, he was sick and tired of all his misery. What was worse, he could see patterns developing. The same things were happening over and over again. The only thing that was different were the people he was dealing with. He always had a boss that was a bully. He always was at odds with the work he did. He always tried to make his girlfriends happy but did the opposite in the end. And he desperately wanted it all to stop.

So what did he do? He turned to books. Freud, Jung, Campbell, Peck, Dyer. The list went on and on. Although each book gave insights and pieces to his internal puzzle, his problems still recurred. At his wit's end, he eventually decided he needed help.

So he bit the bullet and made an appointment to see a psychologist, or more precisely, psychologists.

He went for private sessions, group therapy and even weekend retreats. He discovered there were as many different types of therapists as there were problems. And what was worse, he soon found out, there were some therapists who didn't exactly have their own shit together. For one of them, he felt like he needed a therapist to see his therapist.

However, over the course of time, he did gain some valuable insight. He learned he was an adult child of an alcoholic family, which created bizarre family dynamics and certain behavior patterns. He learned his difficulties around career and money stemmed back to his relationship with his father. He also learned about the enmeshed, stickiness of co-dependency, behavioral tendencies with seemingly good intensions, that eventually doom a relationship.

But still, with all the insight he had gained, psychology seemed a lot like religion. It was a rational approach applied to healing. When his problems came up, he had a fairly reliable internal road map. In fact, he became quite good and recognizing and managing his issues. Nevertheless, his problems never went away. They were still there, repeating over and over again. As much as Jason talked about and analyzed his problems, the more it felt like he was hitting a brick wall. He was afraid he was going to be stuck with his difficulties for the rest of his life. Psychology just couldn't penetrate and heal the depth of what he was feeling inside.

With regret, Jason accepted his fate, and like religion, he left psychology in the rearview mirror.

Nice Ice
It was now three years since Chevron Mountain, Findhorn and Dr. Seymour. With religion and psychology in his past, Jason spiraled to an all-time low. Although he'd gained some awareness and had

been exposed to new ways of thinking, he felt the whole Search-for-Truth thing was a bust. He still had the triangle propped in a sacred spot in his house, where he could see it every day. However, the meaning his visions had provided were depressingly starting to fade. Furthermore, he'd just gone through a prolonged stint of demoralizing unemployment. Times were less than stellar.

Jason moved to a small town in northwestern Montana, where he landed a job in the exploration office of an operating underground mine. It was nowhere near the glitz and buzz of flying around in Alaskan helicopters. Plus, there were some days he had to actually go underground, something he didn't care for at all. It was way too creepy. He disliked it so much, he filed it under "Drudgery and Grind." He would have considered it slave labor, except for one minor detail. He was getting paid.

The town Jason lived in was so small, it didn't even have a decent video store. So in order to fill that gap, he had to drive 15 miles to the next closest town to rent a movie, something he did way more than once.

One lonely winter evening, Jason drove over to rent his favorite movie, *Never Cry Wolf*. He'd seen it a million times but never got tired of it, mostly because it reminded him of Chevron Mountain. On this particular evening, when he walked up to the cashier, he noticed it was a woman in her 50s. Her name tag read Bev. He'd never seen her before. When Jason handed her the rental, she said, "Ah…I love this movie."

"Me too," Jason replied. "It's the only movie I've ever seen that comes close to capturing the spirit of Nature."

That comment certainly caught Bev's attention. She replied, as she rang him up, "If you're interested in the spirit of Nature… here…take this magazine. There's an interesting article about a Japanese researcher…It's somewhere near the middle."

"Thank you. Thank you. I'll read it tonight." Jason said it with such gratitude, Bev wondered if anyone had ever given him anything before.

As soon as he got home, Jason tossed the movie on the kitchen counter and promptly sat down to flip through the magazine. He went straight to the recommended article. It seized and riveted his attention.

It was an article about Masaru Emoto, a Japanese author and entrepreneur, who claimed human consciousness has an effect on the molecular structure of water. His conjecture was that water could react to thoughts and emotions contained in words. There were numerous photos of water crystals, with simple labels on their containers. Words like love, gratitude and peace produced water crystals with beautiful geometric designs, whereas words like hate, envy and greed produce poorly formed, unattractive and deformed crystals.

Jason was glued to the article. He read it several times and studied the photographs for the rest of the evening. That night in bed, he tossed and turned for hours. He couldn't get the water crystals out of his mind. He thought, "If the human body is as much as 75 percent water, then what we think and feel can crystallize." A flash of light ignited his mind. He sprung out of bed and grabbed the triangle. Next, he vigorously searched for Seymour's interpretation of the text. When he found it, he inquisitively read it out loud:

"It is Truth, no lie, certain, and to be depended upon. Human anguish cannot be avoided. Like a serpent chasing its tail, the cycle repeats from within. Learn this and know the soul."

"Yes! That's it!" Jason squealed with delight, like a miner who just struck it rich. "Negative feelings crystallize inside the subconscious emotional psyche. As long as they remain there, pain repeats. That's what the symbol of the serpent represents. No

wonder psychology can't reach deep healing. It's limited to the conscious, analytical mind!"
That night Jason came up with his own lines of text:

"Much of human suffering is caused by crystallized emotions trapped inside. They cause repeating patterns of pain."

Chapter 5
Healing

Vision - The Yogi
When Jason drifted off to sleep that night, his dreams spun out of control. Images and scenes rolled in one after the other—some lucid, some abstract. At one point, he woke up and noticed the sheets were soaked with sweat.

After he dried himself off, he went back to bed and drifted into an even deeper state of sleep. Slowly, like the emergence of dawn, his dreams were filled with soft pastel light. When his awareness was fully lit, Jason found himself standing on the edge of a bluff, overlooking the sea. However, this time he wasn't seeing a vision but was actually in it. The breeze swayed palm trees into a surreal dance, like they were about to dance across the beach. Aroma of the salted air filled his nostrils and the waft of the sea breeze blew through his hair. He sank into a resounding feeling of deep stillness. He took a breath and thought, "Wow, so this is paradise."

From the edge of the bluff, he viewed in the distance a massive, deep kyanite-blue, tropical sea. About a quarter of a mile away from shore, waves were gently breaking on a coral reef. Between the breaking surf and the pristine white-sand beach was the placid backwater of an enormous emerald lagoon. The lagoon stretched about a mile to his right and wrapped around a small mystical looking island.

When Jason had his fill of oceanic bliss, he rotated himself about to get a 360-degree panoramic view. As he turned around, what appeared before him was a traditional Polynesian longhouse, a community building for meetings and prayer. It looked large enough to comfortably hold about 100 people. It had a large thatched roof made from palm tree leaves. The supporting structure was comprised of tightly lashed posts and beams of bamboo. The sliding door was wide open and Jason saw an alter adorned with fresh flowers along the back wall. Between Jason and the longhouse was a large knee-deep pool. It was constantly overflowing with smooth, un-rippled water that looked like moving panes of delicate transparent glass.

As Jason continued to scan the property, he saw the image of a man forming in the center of the longhouse. It was a man from East India who looked like some kind of Yogi or spiritual master. Jason instantly felt drawn toward him. As the alluring feeling intensified, Jason felt the softened eyes of the Yogi fuse with his. Jason also became aware that the Yogi's emotional state was melding with his own. He could feel every emotion the Yogi felt. Or was it the other way around?

Before Jason had time to comprehend what was happening, an overwhelming feeling of sadness rose in his chest. It was unbearable. In moments, he was brought to the edge of tears. However, the Yogi remained unshakably calm and kept his eyes fixed on Jason's. Jason remained observant, even though he was ready to burst into sobs. Then, the Yogi silently levitated in a lotus position. What happened next revolutionized Jason's understanding of emotion.

The Yogi's physical body became transparent and Jason could see layers of colors encapsulating his outline. Jason had heard of auras before but this was the first time he'd actually seen one. Within the gemstone quality of the Yogi's auric colors was a red and very painful looking ball of jagged light. Oddly enough, Jason noticed it was in the same area where he felt the irrepressible sadness in his chest.

Very deliberately, as if he were teaching Jason a lesson, the Yogi closed his eyes. Immediately, the red ball of pain began to slowly spin and take on the shape of a small tornado. As it continued to rotate, Jason saw people and painful events in the vortex. Then, the spinning spiral slowly lifted up and out of the Yogi's body. As it rose above his meditative posture, it began to dissipate, until it transformed into a soft white light. Then it disappeared completely. At the same time, Jason recognized the incredible sadness in his chest had evaporated.

The Yogi repeated the process over and over again, applying the technique to every debilitating emotion imaginable: rage, frustration, unworthiness, loneliness, depression, guilt, and fear. After what seemed like a millennium, the Yogi ended his tutoring session. He opened his eyes and gave Jason the gentlest nod of gratitude. Then without a word, he magically began to dissolve. Jason then understood, the Yogi was the master of his own internal world.

Jason was exhausted from what he considered to be a major emotional workout. His internal body was throbbing like it had been through surgery. After a lengthy while, his pain softened and the pastel light faded. When he awoke, he realized he had been visited by his second spiritual guide.

Excitement
Jason was so excited, he could barely focus on his work the next day. He felt like he had discovered the next Nobel Prize and wanted to shout his epiphany from the rooftops. After work, he drove straight back to the video store to talk to Bev. When he walked in, there she was, filing movies on the shelf. When she saw Jason enter, she grinned like a Cheshire Cat and said, "How was the movie?"

"Oh…," Jason replied, caught a bit off guard. "I didn't watch it… but I've seen if before. The reason I stopped in was to say thanks for the magazine." He stretched out his arm and handed it back. "I read the article you recommended. It gave me some great personal insight."

"Really? You liked it?"

Jason nodded aggressively and said, "Very much. Thank you."

Something suddenly caught Bev's attention. Pausing for a moment, she slowly took a step back and looked directly at Jason, almost as if she were studying something. Although her eyes were gazing in his direction, Jason felt she were looking beyond him—through him.

"Does spirituality interest you?" she asked in a calm but serious tone.

Jason furrowed his brow and innocently replied, "I thought it did for a while but it didn't work out. Quite honestly, I'm not really sure what it is."

"Hmm…" Bev pensively responded. After a few brief and very awkward moments, she said, "I think there's a book you might like. It's called *Autobiography of a Yogi* by Paramahansa Yogananda. He was a Hindu yogi master who traveled extensively throughout America in the early 20th century. One of his teachers was the Hindu saint named Babaji. Over a period of time, Babaji appeared to Yogananda in the flesh, assisting in his evolution and offering guidance in his life's mission. Somehow, I think you'll find his story interesting. I sure did. They have a copy of it at the public library, just a couple of blocks down the street."

Changing the subject, she continued, "If you're interested in trying something new, I have a meditation group that meets every other Wednesday night at my house. There are some wonderful people who attend. You're more than welcome to join us. We'd love to have you."

Jason froze up with a reflex of internal resistance but managed to blurt out, "Thanks for the invite. I'll think about it." As he walked out into the crisp Montana air, he was gently beaming. He felt like he'd just made a new friend.

Triangle Two
It was several days before Jason could make it to the library during open hours. It was a stressful week at work because all he

wanted to do was get his hands on that book. When he finally made it to the library, he went directly to the librarian. She looked it up, wrote down the call number and politely directed, "Downstairs. Take a left. Third isle on your right."

Jason snatched the piece of paper and bolted down the stairs. Within a few seconds, he was standing in front of it. It sat eye-level, slightly pulled out, as if it were waiting for him.

Jason's first glance at the spine told him the book was very old, maybe a copy from the first edition. He cautiously pulled it from the shelf, like he was handling the authentic Holy Grail. As he turned to search for the nearest table, he realized he'd forgotten his much-needed notebook in the truck. "Damn, I better go get it," he muttered in disappointment Reaching up to temporarily re-shelve the book, he gently pushed it back into its original place. However, it wouldn't go back in. There was some kind of obstruction. "The book next to it must have tipped over," he thought. As he reached back to clear the space, he felt it wasn't a book. It was much too small. "Hmm…," he thought, "Maybe a map or some other insert fell out." Slowly, he pulled the obstacle out and noticed it wasn't printed material at all.

When Jason caught a glimpse of the object, his heart skipped a major beat. He stood frozen for at least 15 seconds until he was able to shake himself back into motion. It was another golden triangle. This time, he didn't even look at it but quietly slipped it into his pocket. He felt like the guiltiest spy on the planet. Trying to act nonchalant, he walked upstairs, checked out the book, and made tracks for his truck.

He felt like a bank robber making a getaway. But before making his escape, he stopped by the video store to see Bev. She was delighted to see him again. However, Jason cut through the small talk and pointedly asked, "When's you're next mediation?"

Bev was unsettled by his abruptness, noticing all was not right in his world. Ruffled, she said, "Next Wednesday night at 7:00. Are you alright?"

"Yeah, yeah, I'm okay. Maybe I'll tell you about it next Wednesday." Solemnly, he took down her address with directions and said, "See you next week." Then he flashed a counterfeit grin, turned around, and vanished.

Guide - The Yogi
Jason didn't sleep that night. Instead, he studied the new triangle in microscopic detail. He took numerous photos with a cheap disposable camera and spent hours sketching both sides in precision. He also pulled out his long-forgotten notebook from Anchorage, desperately trying to remember what the Inuit Elder had told him.

The new triangle was nearly identical to the first one. However, there were indentations along the sides instead of tabs. Jason was certain it would fit the first triangle like a glove. When he held the two triangles together, he could feel a magnetic pull. But he didn't want to attach the two, just in case he couldn't pull them apart. He wanted to extract as much detail from the new triangle first.

On the front of the second triangle, there was a symbol in the middle, just like the first triangle. It looked like the Yogi from his dream, levitating in prayer. However, inside his body were seven equally spaced flowers, from top to bottom, along his spine. There were also seven miniature tornadoes, equally spaced, surrounding the Yogi. However, there was no text. The back also had 21 symbols but they were all different than the first triangle. Jason thought he'd seen a couple of them before, somewhere. He also noted, they too, rotated slowly over time.

After Jason documented as much information as he could, he turned to his overflowing notebook from Anchorage. "What did the Elder say, again?" he groused out loud, flipping through the pages. "Here it is…Let's see…You will have guides to help you on your path and teach you spiritual truths. Learn and assimilate the truths to help yourself and others."

Jason guessed finding the triangles revealed some type of progression in his personal growth. The octahedron, from the workshop in Findhorn, was his first guide. It assisted him in learning his first universal truth. "Emotions get trapped inside of people and create suffering." When he came to that awareness, the next triangle appeared. "Maybe I'm headed in the right direction," he thought.

It was about 2:00 a.m. when Jason finished photographing, sketching and gathering information on the second triangle. He made a feeble attempt to get some sleep but it was useless. He was too wired and excited. So he clicked on his night light and grabbed the book Bev had recommended.

His eyes were too tired to read, so he just flipped through the pictures. After about 30 seconds, he was stopped cold. It was a hand-drawn sketch of the saint Babaji, created by Yogananda. Jason immediately hopped out of bed and frantically scrambled for his Anchorage notebook. "Where is that sketch I made?" he pleaded as he rifled through the pages. "There," he said, as he folded the cover back. He held his sketch up to the sketch of Yogananda.

It was a dead ringer.

Babaji was one of the guides who appeared to Jason on Chevron Mountain. He was also in his recent dream, showing him how to release miniature tornados of pain from his aura. It was his image on the front of the second triangle.

"Yes! Yes!" Jason squealed with delight. "It's making sense. Pain gets stuck inside. Meditation must be what releases it. I think I'm getting it!"

He needed some confirmation. It was 3:00 in the morning. Jason figured, if he called now, he might catch Seymour on his lunch break. Luck was on his side because Seymour answered his phone. As expected, Mr. Charisma was delighted of hear from Jason. They joyfully spent the first few minutes of their phone call just catching up.

Seymour had published a no-nonsense scientific paper on the first triangle. He didn't add any metaphysical speculation to his findings. That publication landed him in a feature article of the layman's periodical *Archeology Today*. However, *AT* didn't hesitate to throw in their own theoretical conjunctures. In fact, their article played the paranormal woo-woo card pretty hard. Findhorn, Crop Circles, Stonehenge, Druids, The Great Pyramids: it was all there to go crazy over. That brilliant approach resulted in their best-selling issue ever.

Quite a stir was created in certain British circles for a few months. Seymour was briefly catapulted into the public eye as a minor celebrity. He loved it. It also opened his coffer drawers for more grant funding, to buy a few more photographic toys. Keeping to his word, he kept his mouth shut about Jason. Jason thought that was the best part of all.

Conversely, Jason didn't bother to tell Seymour about his failed search for The Truth. He skipped right over that and went straight for his new discovery. He simply said, "Seymour, I've found a matching triangle."

There was nothing but silence on the other end. Jason thought maybe he lost his connection. "Seymour, are you still there?" he asked.

Seymour cleared his throat and said, "Ah…yes…yes. Let me switch the phone to my other ear. I thought you said you found a matching triangle."

Jason clearly re-asserted, "I did. Why do you think I called? I want to send you some pictures."

"Splendid," Seymour cheered, trying to regain his equilibrium. "Just e-mail some high resolution photos."
"E-what?" Jason miffed.

"E-mail," Seymour retorted. "Electronic mail. It's done with a computer hooked up to the Internet." Then he went on to jabber about photo grains, scanning, resolution, megabytes, JPEG vs. TIF, file size, pixels, etc., etc., etc.

Jason immediately got a headache and his eyes glazed over. "Seymour," Jason protested with a concocted western drawl. "I live in the sticks of northwest Montana, Cowboy. E-mail ain't gonna get here 'fer a while. Besides, out West, we figure technology is way overrated." Jason thought he heard Seymour say something like, "Humph" and then offered to send him professional-grade, color transparencies.

The following weekend, Jason drove 150 miles to the nearest sizable city and had transparency photographs made of the new triangle. A few days later he sent them off via snail mail.

About a week later, Jason received an enthusiastic phone call from Seymour, thanking him for the photos. He indicated the fabrication looked strikingly similar to the first triangle and wouldn't be at all surprised if they were related. However, he guessed the symbols on the back were going to remain a mystery. He also promised another report in the near future. By the time he got off the phone, Seymour was as excited as a little kid. Jason figured Seymour was already planning his first episode on the History Channel, starring none other than himself.

Within a month, Jason was holding a nicely prepared report from Seymour. The report indicated the second triangle was fabricated at the same time and location as the first one, around 2500 B.C. in Egypt.

Furthermore, the seven flowers inside the meditating figure most likely referred to the chakra system. The first documented mentioned of chakras come from the Vedic tradition in India (2000-600 B.C.). Chakras were described as centers of spinning energy located within the human energy field, each relating to different aspects of human consciousness. The small vortexes surrounding the Yogi were most likely related to the chakras. However, Seymour wasn't sure how.

The symbols on the back had Seymour and Higgins baffled. They simply had no historical reference, which meant, they didn't have a clue. They hadn't seen any of them before. Neither had anyone else. At least that's what their research indicated. Furthermore, none of the symbols matched the symbols from the first triangle. However, like the others, they were finely crafted, embedded, 3D glyphs. They had to take Jason's word that the symbols on the second Triangle were also in constant motion.

Bev's Crib
On the day of Bev's meditation group, Jason mailed his transparencies off to Seymour. His head was still reeling from the discovery of the second triangle.

He was very nervous on his way to Bev's house. Even though he'd prayed plenty of times at churches, it was generally a supplication from a laundry list. His zealous religious quest was a desperate attempt to connect to a magnanimous deity outside of himself. However, his preconceived notions of meditation seemed much more unnerving. He thought it was like spying inside of yourself. That was way too personal for Jason. He had no idea what he'd find in there. To be quite honest, he was scared stiff.

When he arrived, he was warmly greeted by Bev. She led him to the meditation room, overlooking the garden. He immediately noticed a painting on the wall of three Arctic Wolves. Another sign. Instantly, he started to relax.

The scent of incense, or some other soothing aroma, gently wafted through the air, creating an atmosphere of safety and tranquility. As he looked around, he saw implements of meditation carefully laid out: crystals bowls, a drum, a rainstick, tuning forks, a few crystals. It was all nicely arranged and adorned, not too whacked out woo-woo. Soft music played in the background that sounded like it was from India.

A handful of participants were already seated. Polite introductions were offered all around. One person was a soft-spoken guy from up near the Canadian border. The rest were local middle-aged women.

Without wasting any time, Bev began the meditation. Everyone was positioned in a semi-circle on comfortable pillows. A couple of folks, including Jason, stretched out on the floor. Bev dimmed the lights and put on some incredible heavenly music. Then, she followed with the soft rhythmic intonations of her own voice.

When Jason lay on the floor, he had no way of knowing this was going to be one of the most pivotal days of his life. Babaji's teachings of inner tornadoes was about to be released. Within moments, Jason would be releasing suppressed emotion, negative thought patterns, and inhibiting beliefs. The monsoons of the past were about to blow through his psyche. Jason later wondered if his insurance company would cover it under "Acts of God."

Floating away on Bev's voice, Jason drifted into a deep state of dreamy relaxation. The fuzziness of his awareness, reminded him of his visions on Chevron Mountain. Slowly, much to Jason's pleasant surprise, Babaji gracefully materialized in his meditation. He was levitating, seated in the lotus position. However, this time he didn't do anything. He was simply there to keep Jason company. It was deeply reassuring.

As Bev guided the group into a deeper trance, Jason's mind started going crazy. "Am I doing this right? I don't feel anything. Is this working?" And so on and so on. About halfway into it, Bev stopped, guided by her intuition. She then walked over to Jason and posed the question of a lifetime (or maybe lifetimes). Keep in mind, Jason and Bev were mere acquaintances. She didn't know anything about him.

The bomb she dropped was, "Jason, what does the word bullying mean to you?" As soon as those words passed her lips, he saw a memory when his boss chewed him out at work, followed by another bully boss. Then, an abusive interrogation during a border crossing; a beating he took from thugs at school; a baseball coach who pushed him down during practice; a teacher who humiliated him in front of his friends; a time his dad ditched him in the woods.

He was hit by the Tidal Wave of Bullying. Every bullying episode he'd ever experienced was launched straight at him, coming in at the speed of a runaway freight train. Furthermore, it wasn't just limited to him. He could see every bullying episode throughout the history of his family.

Shaken to his foundation, tears started to roll, his body convulsed, and images kept zooming in one after the other. He lay there and wept for probably half an hour. It was so embarrassing. After all, he didn't even know these people.

After the meditation ended, Jason was in shock. He made a polite but very hasty retreat. It took him hours to pull himself together. It was obvious he'd stumbled on to some very powerful medicine. But the only question he could come up with was, "What in the world just happened?" He had to know. So he called Bev the next afternoon and asked her out to lunch.

Jason took a couple of days off work, just to rest and stabilize his state of mind. He also continued to read *Autobiography of a Yogi*. By the time he met Bev for lunch, Jason was still pretty shaky. However, he learned she'd taken an intensive meditation training, a few years back. She was by no means an expert but she had a few insights that certainly helped him out.

"During the meditation, you suddenly released pent up emotion from the past. Also, as a group, we set a clear intention for healing to occur. When intention is set, it puts the ball in motion."

Jason thought about that for a few seconds. Yes, he did remember but didn't think much of it at the time.

Bev went on to say, "One thing I've learned about meditation is that once you give it some direction, it will go to work right away. Physical events and circumstances will start happening with uncanny synchronicity. It can be a miraculous wild ride. Based on what you've been through already, I think you'd better buckle your seatbelt."

Jason then told Bev about Chevron Mountain, Findhorn, his search for the Truth, Babaji, and the golden triangles. She was awed and suspected he was a very old soul with a unique life mission.

Without much deliberation, she tenderly said, "Jason, I'm deeply honored to have you attend our little meditations and I hope you continue to come. You are always welcome. However, what we have to offer you is insignificant in the larger scheme of things. You need to develop and learn about yourself, about the gifts you have and the person you are meant to be. There is a school in Fiji, called the Oneness School of Meditation, that teaches advanced meditation techniques. It's the one I went to a few years ago. There are some highly evolved souls who can assist you in your growth. You might want to think about it."

She also said they offered week-long courses almost every month. That put Jason's wheels to turning. He thought he could go the following autumn, after he got laid off. That would give him plenty of time to prepare and save money.

Bye-bye Bully
When Jason returned to work the next day, he heard his Boss (the guy he couldn't stand to be in the same room with), abruptly quit

to take a job with another company. Jason's eyes nearly popped out of his head in surprise. Sheepishly, he sauntered over to his office and peeked inside the door. It was a miracle. His desk was cleared, his pictures removed from the walls. The SOB bully was gone. Jason slowly pushed the door open the rest of the way and stepped inside. It felt like a cargo container full of bricks slid off his back.

"Good God," he said in disbelief. "Is this the result of yesterday's healing meditation?" He felt like dancing. So he did.

Fusion
About two months into his meditations at Bev's, Jason still hadn't fit the triangle pieces together. He was holding off, just in case Seymour wanted more information. However, he eventually hit the point where he couldn't wait any longer. The anticipation was driving him bonkers. Then he had an idea. "I know. I'll put the triangle pieces together at Bev's next mediation." He ran the idea by Bev. She was all over it.

The following Wednesday evening, Jason showed up about an hour early. Bev prepared a stylish table in the middle of the room. Jason carefully unwrapped the triangles and delicately placed them in the center of the table. Bev gasped at first glance and placed the tips of her fingers over her heart. Instinctively, she grabbed a piece of decorative cloth and covered the triangles, as if to safeguard the sacred.

When the rest of the group assembled, Bev gave a brief introduction and turned the floor over to Jason. He was exceptionally nervous and wasn't sure what to say. So, he thought, "What the hell?" and laid it all out. He spilt the entire can of beans: Chevron Mountain, Findhorn, Seymour, Babaji, the works. When he finished, he asked the participants to gather around the table. Then, without another sound, he slowly pulled the cover away.

No one said a word. After about 30 seconds of mesmerized silence, glances started flying around the group. It was the rarest of bondings because they were witnessing the physical manifestation of a genuine miracle.

Jason then asked everyone to return to their seat. He was prepared to fit the pieces together. However, he thought it best if everyone was in a relaxed state first. So he asked Bev to lead a brief introductory meditation. When the group was deeply at peace, Jason calmly stood and walked over to the table. Then, he asked everyone to slowly open their eyes.

Nervously, Jason lifted the two triangles and aligned the tab with the indentation. As he moved the pieces closer together, he felt the magnetic attraction increasing. When they were about two inches apart, the magnetism became too strong for Jason to control. Instantly, they clicked together, flashing an arc of electricity that sent a jolt of energy up Jason's arms. Involuntarily, his entire upper body recoiled and he almost dropped the precious artifact.

What happened next was astounding. Each triangle released a flawless, pitch-perfect tone, similar to tuning forks. Initially, the sounds were barely audible. However, the volume gradually increased over the next several moments. As the timbre intensified, the two sustaining notes created a third overtone, resulting in an immaculate three-part harmony. It was angelic.

Simultaneously, two pulsing orbs of light softly encapsulated each triangle. One was red, the other orange. As the resounding music swelled in volume, the pulsating orbs also expanded. They soon merged into a single sphere of light and completely cocooned the fused triangles. As the luminescence intensified, it transformed into an almost invisible translucent gold. The light became so intense, it started to burn Jason's hands, so he quickly put it down on the table.

Within a few moments, the color and the music faded. Nothing was left, except what was now half of an equilateral pyramid. As Jason inspected it more closely, he noticed the triangles were perfectly fused. There was no residual outline of the tab or the sides of the triangles. Furthermore, the text and the symbol on the front of the first triangle were gone. There was only the outline of the meditative Yogi on the second triangle. Astonished, Jason quickly flipped it over and was glad to see the symbols on the backs were still there. He also noticed the fused triangles were about 75 percent lighter.

No one broke from their open-eyed meditation. Everyone sat deeply relaxed in absolute awe, long after the light and music died out. That was because the fused triangles radiated some type of energy, like gentle tingling sensations. It felt absolutely wonderful. Bev mindfully asked everyone to imagine their deepest fear or pain and to allow the triangles to heal it.

Post Fusion
Two weeks later, at the next meditation, Bev asked people to share their experiences from the previous meeting. It was phenomenal. Everyone experienced a positive shift or healing from the half-pyramid. Steve received an unexpected and sizable inheritance. Fran made peace with her sister. Connie's grueling divorce proceedings came to an unanticipated close. Bev's problem with her knee cleared up. Sue started dating a wonderful new guy. And everyone wanted to do it again.

As for Jason, well, he had the half-pyramid. When he took it home, he noticed he could feel a subtle energy radiating off it all the time.

He cautiously agreed to bring the half-pyramid to one meditation per month, until he left for Fiji. He was more interested in the essence of meditation itself. The half-pyramid seemed like it could become an enormous diversion. Jason didn't want it to become a side-show circus attraction.

A month later, twelve people showed up to the meditation group. Most everyone reported shifts and improvements in their personal lives afterward. However, the healings weren't the Jesus B. Praised kind of miracles. They were more subtle and practical, requiring the participation of each recipient. There were no freebies; they had to engage in their own healing work. However, that requirement didn't stop people from coming to other meditations. On the last one, before Jason left for Fiji, over 100 people showed up.

The cat was out of the bag.

Seymour's Big Mouth
The day after the triangles were fused, Jason called in sick and drove 150 miles to have new transparencies made. He didn't bother notifying Seymour, he just sent the transparencies off with a lengthy hand-written letter.

For the next several weeks, Jason didn't hear a word from Seymour. No phone call, no report...nothing. A week later, he figured it was time to contact Seymour, to see if he had received the photos. That was when the phone rang. It was Liam Perry, a human-interest columnist from the London Times.

Apparently, Seymour submitted a copy of the latest transparencies to the Times, hoping to further launch his narcissistic personality into the limelight. His little ploy backfired. Oh yes, they were interested. They just wanted to see the artifact in person this time. Seymour rolled over like a pig in mud and gave Jason up like a bad habit. The Times contacted Jason within minutes of receiving his contact information. They were also willing to send a reporter to Montana to verify Seymour's research.

Jason vehemently declined their proposal. "Goddamnit, Seymour!" Jason screamed as slammed the phone down. About two seconds later, he was on the phone again, placing a call to the esteemed Dr. Hedgewick. When Seymour spoke with Jason, he discovered his charm wasn't going to cut it, so he backpedaled in an attempt to defend himself. He said he was tricked into letting the information out. Jason knew it was a lie. He knew Seymour was delighted. His attempt at stirring up the pot was a smashing success.

About a month later, Jason received a news clipping from Seymour. He got his article in the Times, front page, Sunday edition, human-interest section. There was a huge photo of Seymour showing off transparencies of the half-pyramid. This time, Higgins and Jason were briefly mentioned in the article.

Now the cat was really out of the bag.

Awareness on the Rise
Until he left for Fiji, Bev did her best to prepare Jason for his upcoming retreat. Her experiences were limited but she noticed he was becoming quite competent at entering deep meditative states. He was also beginning to feel subtle energies associated with his aura. Grateful to see his awareness on the rise, she suspected the half-pyramid was only playing a small role in his development.

As far as healing went, Jason continued to focus on releasing bullies from his subconscious. Bev asked him if he wanted to work on other issues. But he was content to stick with his success with bullies. By the time he left for Fiji, he hadn't had one bullying episode in over six months. Which wasn't bad, seeing how it used to be a steady part of his diet. Of course, unless, constant pestering from Seymour, the London Times, and local news media could be considered bullying.

The Passport
When it finally came time to leave for his retreat, Jason was having second thoughts about going. He was tired of the endless attention he was receiving. Plus, all the hype around the half-pyramid dampened his fire for meditation in general. If that wasn't enough, the exuberant cost of the retreat felt like extortion. With all the extraneous crap flying around in his head, he couldn't have cared less about Fiji.

On the last meditation, the night before Jason left, Bev pulled him aside. She gave him a huge hug, and wished him the very best. "I'll be there, with you in spirit," she said. "Also, be aware. Your internal process will probably begin before you get there." He thanked her from the bottom of his heart and had no idea what she was talking about.

The next day, after depositing the half-pyramid in a safe-deposit box, Jason drove to the nearest sizable town and caught a puddle-jumper flight to Seattle. On the flight over, he was actually toying with the idea of bagging the trip altogether. He thought, "Maybe I'll just go visit some friends up north and do some hiking. Be a hell of a lot less expensive. Fiji? To meditate? I dunno."

Apparently, that didn't sit very well with his higher-self, who wanted Jason's presence whole-heartedly or not at all. He had no way of knowing, but a defining synchronicity was on its way. As Bev mentioned, his process was about to begin.

Jason had a lengthy layover at SeaTac airport. He eventually had to make his way to the terminal of international flights. When he arrived at his gate a few hours before takeoff, there were some airline personal fussing about behind the check-in counter. Two of them were allowing people to check in as they arrived. As Jason approached, he had a knot seize up in his stomach about the size of a basketball. His heart rate shot through the ceiling and he began to sweat. The man at the ticket counter triggered a huge deep-seated fear. He was about six-foot-four, an enormous mass of muscle. His clothes looked uncomfortably tight, which must have contributed to the persistent scowl on his face. He also had a small scar across his cheek and was missing a tooth. His overall persona was…very reptilian. For Jason, it was Dillon McNash the playground bully all over again.

When Jason presented his ticket and passport to the agent, he roared like a dictator, "What? I can't accept this. It's been altered. Did you run this though the washer to blur the photo? I don't know what you're trying to pull here buddy but you'll have to get another one."

Jason was bomb-shelled and timidly defended, "What!?! Another passport? Sir, I've been using this passport for the last three years in Europe and Canada. No one has ever questioned it. You're not even an immigration official. How can you deny me entry into another county?"

Personally affronted, the agent looked across the counter, as if he was about to break Jason's neck and replied, "Listen, this is airline policy. You can get an emergency replacement at the Federal Building. And if you want to get on one of our planes, you will need my personal approval. Furthermore, you better watch yourself. I don't like the way you look. Maybe I should call security." Then he stamped his ticket "rejected," signed his initials, and handed it back to Jason.

Jason turned around and couldn't believe what just happened. "Did he actually say, I don't like the way you look? Geez, all I did was hand him my ticket. What an asshole." He felt like an international felon, accused by someone with absolutely no authority. He also felt like he was about two inches tall.

Jason thought he'd worked hard at healing his issues with bullies but apparently not hard enough. He was no dummy. Now he understood what Bev meant about his process starting before he arrived in Fiji. However, he didn't want to deal with another layer of his peeling onion. His first response was to say, "If this is what the retreat is about, then fuck it. This is too big for me. I need a holiday not a trip through the meat grinder. Plus, it's gonna cost me a new passport, lodging in Seattle, ticket fees and transportation. Hell, that's probably at least 300 bucks. Then I still have to deal with that ticket taker thug, who may not let me on the plane anyway. Hiking up north sounds pretty good."

The retreat was still two days off. If Jason was lucky, he could get an emergency passport from the federal building in downtown Seattle. Or he could just bag it and head north. He had a choice to make. He could make the effort or simply blow it off. After pissing and moaning in the airport for a about an hour, he sucked it up and decided to go. With that decision and intention established, he was set up for one of the wildest rides of his life.

He grabbed a cab and checked into a hotel, a few blocks from the Federal Building. His room was the Grizzly Room, decorated with teddy bears. It was his totem Bubba from Alaska. There were also some travel brochures from Fiji. Trying to reassure himself, he thought, "That's two good signs…I'll take it."

He spent the rest of his evening attempting to calm down, by releasing bullies from inside his body.

He got the only opening for emergency passports the next morning at 8:00 a.m. As soon as the ink dried from the rubber stamp, Jason made a straight shot for the airport, with no time to spare. When he approached the ticket counter, he was greeted by a very attractive young woman about his age. They both exchanged innocent glances and were a bit giggly when he handed her his ticket. Jason went on to explain, he needed approval from General A-hole, based on the previous day's encounter. She took his ticket and politely indicted the manager in question no longer worked for the airline. He could board as soon as his row number was called.

"Wow," Jason thought. "I guess the meditation is working. No bully and a cute chick to boot; double whammy."

Oneness School of Meditation
Jason's flight to Fiji was delayed by three flat tires: the airplane, the taxi to the bus station, and the bus to the retreat. The flat tire on the bus was caused by driving for an hour with the emergency brake on. The rim of the tire got so hot, it cracked. Because the bus was full of spiritually-oriented women and an inept bus driver, Jason had to fix the flat by himself. After fixing the tire, Jason wondered what type of meaningful symbolism the flat tires held. He didn't like what he came up with, so he tried not to think about it.

When they arrived at the retreat center, they were greeted by native Fijians singing a traditional welcome song. It was so beautiful, it sent a warm tingle through Jason's heart. He hopefully thought, "Maybe all the crap over the last two days was worth it."

The Oneness School of Meditation was based out of India. However, these classes were being held at their satellite campus in Fiji. It was a high-end resort, owned by an American celebrity Jason had never heard of. As soon as everyone piled off the bus, they were directed straight to check-in. The first gathering in the community lodge wouldn't be until evening. That gave the guests plenty of time to settle in and get acquainted.

Jason got himself situated and immediately went for a long stroll on the beach. The last two days were a bit grueling; all he wanted to do was unwind by himself. So he walked and rested until early evening, making his way over to the lodge in time for the first meeting. When he stepped inside, he couldn't believe his eyes. It was the bamboo longhouse from his vision on Chevron Mountain. The sliding doors were wide open with an incredible view of an overflowing pool, a lagoon, and a distant reef. It was paradise all over again.

There were 32 people attending the retreat, mostly Westerners. Much of the teaching would be done in the community lodge. However, four smaller break-out groups met daily for intimate discussion and personalized instruction. The teachers leading the small groups were a woman from Australia, a husband and wife couple from Fiji, and a man from India, named Anandaji.

Anandaji looked exactly like Jason's visions of Babaji. Jason's eyes quickly flashed around the room to see if anyone was as flabbergasted as he was. As far as he could tell, it didn't look like it. What was even better, Jason would be having several one-on-one meetings with Anandaji throughout the week. The first one was slated for the next day, immediately after breakfast. He couldn't wait.

Jason went to bed that night, disconcerted by the surreal events of the last two days. He felt like he'd wandered into a time/dimension warp and found it difficult to get to sleep. When he finally drifted off for the night, his body sharply twitched. He twitched so hard it woke him up. It twitched again. Fifteen minutes later, he was in full-blown convulsions. It took another 15 minutes for the spasms to finally stop. "Geez," he thought to himself, "are the exorcisms starting already? The retreat doesn't officially begin until tomorrow. I guess I'm getting my money's worth." With that last thought, exhaustion carried him off to sleep.

Kundalini

In the morning, Jason was worried about what happened the night before and wondered if he should see a doctor. However, there was so much he wanted to say to Anandaji, he figured his health could wait. He desperately wanted to know if Anandaji was really Babaji.

Anandaji was already seated in a lotus position, in a large overstuffed chair, when Jason entered the room. He was dressed in simple white clothes, simultaneously exuding the presence of an ancient guru and an impish child. Jason couldn't believe how young he looked. It seemed he was in his early twenties but Jason suspected he was much older. Regardless, Jason couldn't get the question out of his head, "How can he teach meditation? He's too young. There are people here two or three times his age. He can't have more wisdom than them."

When Jason entered and sat down, he could barely contain himself. He was excited, nervous, and eager to learn. But more than anything, he wanted to tell Anandaji everything he'd been through over the last three years. He desperately yearned for advice from an expert.

Just as Jason was about to spew his life story, Anandaji beamed an ear-to-ear grin and gently waved his hand, as if he were shooing a fly. Then he said in the softest of East Indian accents, "Jason, my dear friend. Please relax. I've been awaiting your arrival for some time. I know of your discovery, your mystical visions, and the influential people you have met. I have also glimpsed into your future and know where your path may be leading you. But let's not worry ourselves about the past or the future. Our goal this week will be to focus on right now, the present. So please do not worry. You have come to the right place. You are in good hands. God has brought me here to help you."

Jason just sat there stupefied, silenced in mid-thought. Anandaji, recognized Jason's perplexity and politely inquired, "And how were your travels?" Jason laughed at the absurdity of the question and told him about his mishaps with his passport, the flat tires and his seizure. Anandaji snickered with delight and said, "This is wonderful news!" Jason didn't think so and asked why. Anandaji replied, "Your electrical system is being rewired. It's the first necessary step in your evolutionary process. It's why you are here. Oh, what a fine student you are!"

Jason eyes glazed over as if Anandaji were speaking in Martian.

Intuitively puzzled, Anandaji lightly strained his face and said, "Let's keep this first meeting simple. Words will only confuse things." Then he stood up and walked over to Jason and placed his left hand behind his head. With the middle finger of his right hand, he tenderly touched his third eye, between his eyebrows. From that moment on, he didn't say another word.

Jason immediately felt a slow, controlled explosion of energy creeping up from the base of his spine. It was warm, brilliant energy. It moved up his back and encapsulated his entire body. He felt like his entire aura was glowing but he didn't see any light; it was all feeling. Next, he was overtaken by a sensation he guessed to be euphoria. He'd never felt anything like it.

After a few minutes, Anandaji lowered his hands and left the room. Jason was left by himself to assimilate the experience. At first, he noticed he could see everything in crystal-clear 3D. Then, he noticed all of his senses were heightened. He could smell the fragrant flowers down by the beach, over a quarter of a mile away. At lunch, he could taste every heavenly ingredient in the meal.

That evening, he heard fruit bats flying around that were supposedly silent. And his awareness of touch was aroused beyond belief. Much to Jason's pleasant surprise, his heightened sensory awareness remained active for the entire retreat. When he returned home, he continued to drift in and out of it over the next six weeks.

A few minutes after Anandaji exited, Jason slowly wandered back to his room. He was trying to adjust to his altered state of awareness. When he arrived, he unlocked the door and reached for the light switch. As soon as he flipped it on, the overhead light exploded into a thousand pieces, shooting glass shrapnel all over the place. Jason dashed outside and ran to the front office to contact maintenance.

Over the course of the day, Jason was blowing out electrical equipment everywhere he went. The heating trays at lunch all fritzed out when he walk into the dining room. A fire alarm went off when he entered the exercise room. Three car alarms triggered when he passed by a parking area. By the end of the first day, he had already developed a reputation. At the meditation that evening, Anandaji had Jason enter and exit the community lodge several times, just to watch the circuit breakers flip. Jason was becoming a regular electrical vaudeville act.

Electricity wasn't the only thing bursting out of Jason's aura. His sex drive skyrocketed off the chart. Two-thirds of the participants at the retreat were women and he was having fantasies about all of them. He had to take three cold showers a day just to keep himself in check. It was a very, very difficult energy to constrain.

On the third day of the retreat, Jason had another personal meeting with Anandaji. Before Jason had a chance to sit down, Anandaji asked with a laugh, "So, how are your sexual urges?" Embarrassed, Jason went on to explain he could barely contain himself. He was certain it was going to get him into trouble.

Anandaji went on to articulate, "What you are experiencing, my good friend, is called the Kundalini. In India, the Kundalini is historically referred to as a rising serpent. It can arise at the beginning of a spiritual awakening. The stored energy in the base of your spine has been released, aggressively awakening the rest of your energy. The electrical outages you are causing are also due to the ascending Kundalini."

Anandaji continued, "To maximize use of your sexual energy, here is what I suggest you do. The next time you feel sexually aroused, sit in meditation. Then, focus your attention on the sexual energy alone. Try not to focus on your fantasies. That is all you need to do. This will give you permanent access to your newly available energy. Give it a try, see what happens!"

Two hours later, that's exactly what Jason did. When the next wave of erotic vigor growled in his loins, he used every ounce of his will to ignore his fantasies. Then, he sat down, closed his eyes, and focused his attention squarely on the sexual energy. Immediately, the ball of energy blazing in his pelvis began to intensify and expand. Jason also felt his heart rate surge. Perspiration rolled down from his armpits. Like a weightlifter focused on his weights, Jason kept his attention riveted on the energy. It was everything he could do to hold it back.

Then, in the blink of an eye, the sphere of vitality exploded and shot a beam of light through the top of his head, straight toward heaven. A similar beam of light blasted toward the center of the Earth. Instantly, he was catapulted into an extraordinary realm of perception. For a few moments, he felt like the most powerful person in the world. Holding his focus, he basked in the intense column of light until it faded. Afterward, he felt like he'd been completely reworked from the inside out. Jason didn't know it but he'd never be the same again.

The Tiger
To enhance experiences like kundalini awakenings, the courses of the retreat focused on specific themes for each day, such as relax-

ation, healing, and visualization. Accompanying each daily theme were lectures, introductions to techniques, discussions, and meditations. Although there was plenty of free time for reflection, the schedule was quite demanding.

On the last full day of the retreat, the theme for the day was fear. More specifically, overwhelming fear. The technique Anandaji introduced to handle overwhelming fear was called "Catching the Tiger by the Tail." It was to be used only when all of the other meditation methods had failed. It was daring, effective, and beautiful in its simplicity.

Anandaji went on to say, "Overpowering fear, such as horror or anxiety attacks, are extreme emotions based on past events. They are the Tiger. The Tiger shows up when everything else stops. Maybe you're unemployed. Maybe your children have moved out to begin their own lives. Maybe you are ill or injured. Whatever the circumstance, it ends up with you being all alone with your fear, that is…the Tiger. And the Tiger can be enormous. In fact, it can be more than you can handle.

"So what do you do? Meditation doesn't work. Visualizations don't work. Praying doesn't work. Psychology doesn't work. And pills certainly don't work. What, then, do you do? Here is what you do: You grab the Tiger by the tail and let it devour you.

"However, if you choose this courageous path, do it with absolute conviction and intention of healing the fear completely. Then, step into the fear and let it take you: body, mind and soul. This will be one of the greatest acts of courage you will ever perform in this life because you will be consumed by your fear. Furthermore, you will not know the outcome and the process may last for days. However, in terms of personal growth, it is absolutely necessary. Because in order to evolve, you must face your own fear.

"Eventually, the fear will subside and you will understand a basic human truth. Fear is a smokescreen, an illusion based on memories of past events. Most fear is not even real and the only way to understand that is to step into it."

*

After Anandaji's lecture, he led the entire group through a visualization to release fear. As the meditation began, Jason was unable to relax. His imagination was fuzzy at best. He came up with his father (again) and a bullying episode from the past. However, he'd been through all that a number of times at Bev's meditations. As he struggled to meditate, he wondered, "How many times do I have to rehash this garbage?" He simply wasn't getting into the zone.

After about ten minutes of mussing around and getting nowhere, Jason got up and walked toward the door. On his way out, Anandaji gave Jason an enormous toothy smile. He then bowed his head, and gently joined his hands in prayer position as if to say, "Namaste." Jason grinned and nodded in acknowledgement, then quietly slipped out the door.

Over the past week, Jason had heard miraculous stories of a waterfall and cave about two miles away. He desperately wanted to see them before he headed back home. Since he'd just created a hole in his schedule, he figured it was as good of a time as any and set off for a little exploration adventure.

He walked at a brisk pace and arrived in about half an hour. The two-tiered waterfall was nestled into a tropical paradise. Crystal-clear pools captured the falling water in an ambience of tranquility, enhanced by the fragrance and color of dangling ferns and orchids. Jason saw the cave above the falls. From his vantage point, it looked more like a grotto than a cave. Nonetheless, he had to check it out and decided that would be his first stop. However, after a brief inspection, he realized there wasn't a well-worn trail. It was a moderately difficult scramble to reach the entrance.

He took his time and slowly worked his way up and into the cave, stepping over rocks and debris as he went. He had no desire of going into the deep darkness. However, the entrance to the cave was so large, he'd be able to go quite a ways and still have light.

Jason made it about 200 feet and decided that was far enough. He also realized it was the end of the cave. Cautiously, he turned around and peered at the cave entrance. At that distance, it was about the size of his thumbnail. Enjoying the silence and solitude of the dark, he thought he'd sit and capture the stillness for a few moments. As soon as his butt hit the ground, he saw a silhouette in the entrance of the cave. "Hmm…," he thought. "Maybe someone from the retreat is looking for me. I better head back."

As he slowly worked his way through the darkness, he saw the silhouette wasn't human. It was a four-legged animal. A bolt of panic shot through his heart. He didn't feel safe. His mind unhinged, "Is it a feral dog? A wild donkey? A wild boar?" He didn't know what to do. He froze and hoped whatever it was would go away.

As he waited in silence, his fear escalated into a full-blown anxiety attack. Suddenly, there in the darkness, he saw memories of his father, his grandfather and countless other tyrants he had known. "No!" he screamed to himself. "This fear with bullies has got to stop!" He guessed he was having another surreal vision, like on Chevron Mountain. So he mounted his courage to "Catch the Tiger by the Tail," and approached the beast in the entrance, hoping to conquer the manifestation of his inner fears. When he was within a few yards of the entrance, the beast stood and blocked the light. It was massive grizzly bear.

"Haa!" Jason screamed with the hubris of power, as he recognized his animal totem. "There are no bears in Fiji! This is a dream to make me face my fear!" However, in the back of his mind, he self-consciously noticed it didn't feel like a dream. It felt like real-time, normal life. Ignoring that faint intuition, he fixed his stance, summoned his bravery, and stood his ground. The bear, in response, dropped to all fours and slowly stalked Jason, clicking its teeth, drooling, and shaking its head from side to side. Jason froze like a deer in the headlights. His heart sank like a bomb, as he realized this was no vision. This was real.

Before Jason had time to think, the bear charged and smacked him alongside the head, knocking him nearly unconscious. Then, it pinned him down flat on his back, with an enormous paw on his chest. Using its immense weight as leverage, the bear sunk its teeth into Jason's arm and pulled it clean out of the socket. Jason screeched in terminal horror. As if to silence the annoying screams, the bears grabbed Jason by the neck and shook him like a rag doll.

Everything went silent and black.

*

When Jason regained consciousness, he was standing unharmed and chest-deep in the upper pool of the waterfall. Calm but exhausted, had no idea how he got there. He also didn't have any strength left to care. He had given up completely. Given up on trying to heal, given up on trying to make sense of things, given up on giving up. He was spent, played out.

Limply gazing into the transparent water below, he saw images drifting out of his body. There were scenes from his childhood: horror, fear, victimhood, self-consciousness. The pool was absorbing the memories out of his body, like water on a paper towel. One by one, the images effortlessly drifted across the surface of the pool and fell over the lower waterfall. Jason worked his way over to the edge to see where they'd gone. From there, he saw his past exploding into the pool below, forming every color of the rainbow.

When the last image burst into fireworks, Jason crawled out of the pool and began his slow trek back down to the retreat. As he ambled down the trail, he noticed he felt lighter. Not only was his heart lighter, from the release of an enormous emotional burden, but his body felt lighter. He felt like he'd lost about 10 pounds.

About half way into his return, he sensed something like wispy clouds. He couldn't see them but felt them. They moved in, out, around, and through his body. The sensations were subtle but the more he focused his attention on them, the more he knew they were real. In the pool a veil had been lifted, allowing him to sense his own energy field.

When he finally arrived at the retreat, the meditation in the longhouse was just letting out. Students were trickling out a few at a time. When Jason neared the main entrance, Anandaji stepped out, accompanied by a fellow instructor.

When they passed each other, Anandaji sparkled a grin at Jason. Without stopping, he said, "Did you catch your Tiger, I mean Bear, by its tail?"

Jason just shook his head in amazement, grinned as he passed, and didn't say a word.

Anandaji turned back over his shoulder and called out, "Don't forget. Last meeting tomorrow. After breakfast."

Anandaji Speaks
Jason skipped breakfast the next morning, anticipating his final meeting with Anandaji. He was so excited, he arrived 15 minutes early. When Anandaji entered, he looked spry and refreshed as usual. Jason wondered if he ever slept or ate. Anandaji then proceeded to seat himself, as if he were floating above his chair, and politely asked, "How has your week been, my friend?"

Jason erupted into a discourse of the cave incident, in detail. He also went on at length about the half-pyramid, Bev, Chevron Mountain and his visions, unloading everything he'd been holding inside. Anandaji sat and simply nodded with deep interest, interjecting an occasional grin. When Jason finished dumping his millstone, he looked squarely at Anandaji and asked, "How do you know so much about me? Are you some kind of mind reader?"

Anandaji chuckled and replied, "Oh my, heavens no! I'm not nearly that invasive. You see Jason, I'm an old soul from both the past and the future, funneled through my existence here in the present. I have also developed an abundance of spiritual skills over the course of many lifetimes. In this life, my mission is not focused on myself or my development. I'm here to help others, such as yourself, in the evolution of their souls. I am, therefore, at your service."

Anandaji continued. "Jason, when you first arrived, I knew you were a superior student. However, over the course of this week, you have wonderfully surpassed my expectations. During the past few days, you have acquired the skills of a healer. All you need to do now is implement those skills into your life when you return home. I also suspect you will evolve into a spiritual warrior. But don't concern yourself with that now. You still have many experiences to assimilate and decisions to make before then.

"This week you have completely grasped the first step toward spiritual proficiency. You have skillfully digested the techniques of releasing stuck emotions, rigid thought patterns, and outdated beliefs. Every saint and ascended master, throughout history, has perfected the art of mastering their emotional and mental states. However, I was surprised to see you take it one step further.

"Through your experience with the bear in the cave, you not only comprehended, but actually implemented, the art of surrender. As you grow from an emotional being to a spiritual being, you will learn the absolute necessity of that act. Surrender is the cornerstone of spiritual enlightenment. Your experience in the pool has already set the tone for your awakening. But again, don't worry about that now. That is still many years away. However, the memory created in the pool will come back to you, if you ever need it."

Jason was confused and inquired, "How long does it take to release suppressed emotion and clear out the mind? There seems to be so much garbage in there. I feel like it will take forever."

Anandaji replied with a seriousness that conveyed he'd experienced the same problem himself. "We all have emotions from the past stuck inside. As we learn to allow them to pass through us, they are permanently released. It's like burning a log. At first, the log may not burn all the way. But with each subsequent fire, the log will eventually be reduced to ash. As you release repeating stuck emotions, they will decrease in their intensity and frequency of occurrence over time. Eventually, they will be gone completely. With awareness, they can all be released over the course of a single lifetime."

"What happens when all the stuck emotions are gone?" Jason asked.

Anandaji squealed with delight and said, "You will find out, my friend! It's called Awakening! It's the only reason we exist. We are here to wake up!"

With that said, the time came for Anandaji and Jason to part, as best of friends. However, Jason was deeply saddened and was very reluctant to say good-bye.

"Do not despair my friend, we have not seen the last of each other yet," Anandaji said.

With that final bit of encouragement, teacher and student vigorously shook hands and bid each other an affectionate farewell. However, as soon as their hands clasped, Jason was catapulted into a severely altered state of consciousness.

Vision - The Madonnas
Jason's heart immediately started throbbing. It also began to expanded like a balloon. As the throbbing intensified, a fissure slowly ripped open. Jason reeled at the resulting gash and was

thrust into a bottomless pit of anguish. It felt like his heart was torn out of his chest.

When all felt lost, Jason's senses were inundated with a magnificent aroma. It was the smell of fresh, wild mountain roses. It reminded Jason of driving along the Columbia River near the Canadian border, on a beautiful warm evening in June. He felt the breeze flowing through his hair, as he imagined himself cruising down a trafficless highway with the windows wide open. It was a rose infused nirvana.

He was baffled by the paradox of an aching heart and the overwhelming perfume of roses.

Jason squinted his eyes, as new images glowed into view. Two breathtakingly beautiful women slowly came into focus. They weren't normal women but Madonnas, radiating a love that could only come from deities. They reminded Jason of Mother Mary, from Sunday school. One was with a Joseph-type husband and the other was carrying a baby Jesus.

Engrossed in their presence, Jason intuitively knew they were there for his healing. They came to heal his broken heart. Suddenly, a shudder of trepidation shot through his awareness. "Is my heart going to be broken? Twice?" As soon as that perception darted through, each of the Madonnas softly repeated, "Remember, we are always there for you. Remember, we are always there for you."

As the Madonnas began to fade, a bottomless hole formed in the pit of Jason's heart. "No!...Wait!...Please don't go!...Don't go!" he pleaded. Heedless to his calls of distress, they slowly melted away, replaced by two distinct scenes. One was a majestic mountain canyon, with waterfalls cascading over vertical walls. The other was a simple cobble beach, along a pristine whitewater river. Jason strained to memorized the views, knowing he'd see them again one day. Within a few moments, the beautiful scenes also began dissolve. Jason desperately tried to cling to the moment, by taking a deep inhalation of the fading rose perfume. By the time everything vanished into the cosmos, he knew he had just met his third spiritual guide.

A few moments later, when Jason came back into full conscious awareness, he was in his room with his packed bags. He had no idea where Anandaji was.

Triangle Three
On his return journey, Jason had plenty of time to reflect. He contemplated the numerous healing techniques he'd experienced, including how meditation can facilitate freedom from the past. He was amazed how one brief week on a remote tropical island could permanently heal difficulties psychology couldn't touch. He couldn't wait to practice them on himself and his friends.

When Jason arrived back home, there was another stack of mail waiting for him. He tossed his bag on the couch and started flipping through the envelopes of junk and bills. However, one large envelope stood out from the rest. It was an A5 international mailer with no return address. He flipped it over. Oddly, there was no postmark on it either. "Seymour?" he thought. "Anandaji? Nah, couldn't be." Using his finger as a letter opener, he quickly tore it open. Sandwiched between two pieces of foam core was another golden triangle. Shocked, he carefully set it down on the kitchen table.

This triangle was slightly different from the first two. It was the same size but noticeably thinner. Jason suspected it was solid gold because it seemed too slight to have a wooden core. Furthermore, there was no script or text. Etched on the front were two interlocking symbols that he immediately recognized. They were the glyphs of Venus and Mars. Jason also knew they represent woman and man, respectively. Venus was a circle with a cross extending from the bottom, making it look like a human stick-figure. Mars was a circle with an arrow extending from the two o'clock position. Both circles were linked, like the circles on an Olympic flag. And like the other triangles, there were 21 symbols on the back, all unknown to Jason. Continuing to scrutinize the details, he noticed he could not only feel, but also faintly see, some type of energy pulsing off its edges.

Again, he sketched it in detail and borrowed a camera from a friend to snap some photos. No transparencies this time and certainly no Seymour. Jason was fed up with the attention the other triangles had received. This time, it was going to be strictly hush-hush.

As soon as he gathered all the information he wanted, he went straight to his safe-deposit box and grabbed the half-pyramid. That evening he arranged an impromptu alter, burned a little incense, and drifted into meditative state. Then, he picked up the half-pyramid and the third triangle and fitted them together.

This time, there was no magnetic pull or shock of electricity. Instead, the entire room was filled with a breathtaking fragrance of wild roses, as a warm glow enveloped Jason's hands. Immediately, it triggered his memory of the two Madonnas from Chevron Mountain. Slowly and gently the glow worked its way up his arms, into the center of his chest, creating a sensation of unlimited love. Tears tenderly started to flow. Then the triangle seamlessly joined with the half-pyramid, as the etching of the Yogi vanished. Only the symbols of Venus and Mars remained on the three fused triangles.

Jason suspected he'd learned a universal truth about meditation and healing. He hoped the arrival of the new triangle meant he was ready to learn his next truth. It had been three years between the emergence of the first and second triangles. The third triangle arrived in a matter of months. He was ecstatic to think his soul evolution was on an exponential trajectory. He was confident he'd knock out the Venus and Mars lesson in no time flat.

Chapter 6
Relationship

Bye-bye Montana

When Jason returned home from Fiji, he soon realized the relationship with his girlfriend wasn't the same. They'd been seeing each other for about six months and talked about moving in together before he left. Although they shared a few things in common, it wasn't their mutually shared passions that brought them together. She had a love for horses that was as foreign to Jason as Chinese calligraphy. She was also pretty ambivalent about his zeal for meditation. She figured he'd get over it soon enough. In all honestly, their relationship was mostly born out of loneliness and physical attraction.

It didn't take long until they were fighting all the time. Jason realized his neediness, the fuel that brought them together in the first place, had been healed. With the neediness gone, so was the basis for their relationship. They just weren't on the same page anymore. It didn't take her long to find somebody else.

After she left, Jason remembered a teaching from Anandaji. He didn't understand it at the time but it was a forewarning. It went something like this:

"Sometimes, when a person goes through a growth spurt of awareness, the energy dynamics in a close personal relationship can change. If both people aren't growing at the same rate, it can be like joining opposite ends of a magnet. Unfortunately, after a retreat of this nature, it's not uncommon for some couples to split up."

Within one month, Jason was single and unemployed. Furthermore, he'd outgrown the meditation at Bev's, as she predicted he would. Plus, he kept running into his ex-girlfriend and his former "buddy" she was sleeping with. After seeing them together at a few social events, he asked himself, "Why am I torturing myself like this?" The more he thought about it, the more he couldn't come up with a good answer. It was obvious. It was time to leave.

Two weeks later, Jason was packed up and waving good-bye to Montana. Next stop—Washington State. Back to the land of salt water, evergreens and Mom's home cookin'. He also put the three-quarter pyramid in storage and left it there for quite a while.

As soon as Jason unpacked his bags in Washington, he was contacting old friends and volunteering them for free healing sessions. Over a several year period he helped people overcome a variety of challenges including fibromyalgia, anxiety attacks and all sorts of emotional difficulties. It turned out to be the perfect place to successfully pay his dues and hone his healing chops.

Manifesting
To stay on top of his healing vocation, Jason did a fair amount of reading and attended continuing education workshops from time to time. One workshop he attended was entitled, "Visualization and the Art of Manifesting."

According to the instructor, manifesting was a spiritual skill. Through meditation, the imagination can direct the subconscious mind to create the future. When a mental picture (vision) gets combined with a deep feeling of "knowing" (confidence), the subconscious mind will do everything in its power to create it. The teacher said it could be applied to all aspects of life. Jason wondered if it could cook up a new relationship.

He'd been single since moving back to Washington and was in the final stages of licking his wounds from the Montana Mess, as he called it. He thought it might be time to throw his hat back in the ring. So, immediately after the workshop, he tried his luck at manifesting a new girlfriend.

Jason's manifesting meditations created an intricate story that unfolded over the course of eight months. During his first meditation, he found himself in the Swedish countryside. He could see everything in minute detail. There was a brick house, an arched doorway, a tile living room with an intricate inlay of a nautical compass, a barn and an enormous sycamore tree in the back. Jason had a fair hand for illustration, so he was able to draw most of it in reasonable detail.

With each progressive meditation, the story added more and more pieces to the puzzle. There was an attractive, auburn-headed woman living in the house. She had all the bounce of an athlete and Jason knew she was his next mate. He also had a gnawing suspicion they'd known each other before in previous lifetimes. There was also her endeared aunt, referred to as Mama, who had a Buddha belly, big brown eyes, and a gray Victorian curls.

Jason became so enamored with his visions, he finally decided they were real. His next reasonable step was to go to Sweden and find out. So he packed up his drawings, took them along as life maps, and dragged a friend along to chauffeur.

Jason thought his new love awaited near a small town in north-central Sweden, at the south end of a large glacial lake. After doing a little map dowsing, he decided the town best fitting his visions was a village named Storuman. So off he went, to the hinterlands of Scandinavia.

After four plane flights and some incredible jet lag, they reached the northern woods of Sweden. Unfortunately, as they drove through the rolling hills on that October morning, they couldn't see a thing. It was a fog thicker than pea soup. The visibility was less than 100 yards at best. Jason was completely crestfallen. He knew they'd come a long way for nothing.

"How could I be so stupid and follow such an idiotic pipe dream?" he chastised himself. "I must be out of my mind."

However, as they pressed on and crested a hill, a break in the clouds framed the area of destiny. "There!" he screamed. "Stop!"

They pulled off the road and Jason dug out one of his drawings. It was identical. Jason's traveling companion couldn't believe his eyes. They climbed back in and slowly pulled into town, taking a turn here and another one there, following the drawing and the memory of Jason's visions. When they reached the suspected destination, there was no house, no gigantic sycamore. It was just a thicket of pine trees. However, it looked like a fire had roared through the area sometime long ago.

They got out and rummaged around. Sure enough, there was brick rubble from an old building. Upon closer observation, they sussed out a floor that included an intricate inlay of a nautical compass. Jason suspected from that moment on, his eight months of meditation were scenes from a past life. After that realization set in, he became very dejected. All he wanted to do was go back home.

When he returned, Jason gave up on manifesting and settled into the more boring world of "real life." He also started dating again. However, each woman he dated brought up similar feelings from old relationships. They weren't like the Montana Mess. That whole episode was shallow and mostly physical. These feelings were much deeper and permeated every relationship he'd ever been in, including with his parents. He called them "sucky, enmeshed and co-dependent." So he quit dating altogether and made an appointment to see a healer he knew, intent on healing himself instead. He was sick and tired of the whole boy-girl business.

Pia and Peanut
A few days after his session with the healer, Jason went to the weekly farmer's market down by the bay. It was a delightful outdoor venue, held every Saturday. He didn't have an agenda and was just killing time, enjoying the crowd and a beautiful autumn day. He'd just picked up a coffee and was adding a little cream,

when he heard from behind, "Hey, Jason!" It was Gloria, Jonathan's former girlfriend. He hadn't seen her in years.

As they joyfully greeted, Jason saw Gloria wasn't alone. Jason thought he knew Gloria's companion from somewhere but couldn't quite place it. After a few moments of small talk, Gloria turned and introduced her friend, "Jason, this is Pia. She's from Sweden."

In the middle of his next breath, Jason's world skidded to an abrupt halt. He recognized Pia immediately. She was the auburn-headed athlete from his manifestation meditations. She also had an 18-month-old baby girl, named Peanut, bouncing on her hip. The little rodent had a miniature Buddha belly, big brown eyes, and Victorian curls.

Jason didn't know what to say. So he didn't say anything…at first. He just stood there with his mouth hanging open. When he finally said something, he stammered incoherently like a total idiot. It didn't take long for the conversation to awkwardly fizzle out. Within a few minutes of meeting, the three of them wandered off and disappeared into the crowd.

Jason spent the rest of the day kicking himself, saying, "How could you be so stupid? You just let her walk off. Destiny slipped right through your finger tips. What is your problem? How chicken can you get?"

Over the next few days, Jason talked himself into the idea: If he was meant to be with Pia, they'd meet again. He was faithfully turning his destiny over to a higher power. Or maybe, it was wishful thinking to justify his cowardice at the moment of opportunity. Whatever the case, it didn't matter because he'd done everything in his power to contact Gloria. She was nowhere to be found. It was like she vanished from the face of the Earth.

About a month later, Jason was sitting in the cafe attached to the local food co-op, still grousing about his missed opportunity with

Pia. Between sips on his latte, he looked up. At the far end of the store, Pia was pushing Peanut around in a shopping cart.

Jason saw it as a supreme sign from on high and immediately raced down the adjacent isle. He nonchalantly turned the corner and pretended he was shopping. "Pia!" he proclaimed, trying to act surprised. "Nice to see you. I thought you went back to Sweden."

"Hi, Jason!" she replied, with a sparkle in her eye. "Oh, no. I live here, at least for now."

After exchanging a little playful banter, Jason invited them over to his table. Two hours later, they were still there, chattering away.

Pia left Sweden several years ago to travel the world with a friend. They bounced the globe from ski town to ski town, visiting the likes of New Zealand, Canada and many points in between. On one of her side excursions to Alaska, she met a Native Alaskan man and got pregnant. A brief marriage ensued resulting in two highly prized possessions: 1) an American green card and 2) Peanut. Pia was more or less biding her time and working as a nurse when she met Jason.

Jason unloaded most of his life story on Pia that day with one exception; he didn't tell her about the three-quarter pyramid. For some reason he never fully understood, he felt compelled to withhold that information. Years later, he'd reflect, "I guess it just wasn't part of her story."

Within two years, they were married with a bouncing family of three (actually six, if you count the hamster, the rabbit and the dog). From then on, it was all about marriage, family and work. Jason was amazed how time consuming it was. He was stretched beyond what he thought possible, learning patience, tolerance, compromise and thinking about other people first. Any spare time was reserved for sacred outdoor play, something both Jason and Pia enjoyed.

However, as the years slipped by, Jason's reflective time was severely compromised. He squeezed in a scant amount of healing work but his personal meditation time was practically nil. He simply didn't have the energy. He begrudgingly surrendered to the fact that parenting was what Buddhists referred to as dharma. It was an active meditation, a spiritual practice in and of itself.

On rare occasions, like when Pia went back to visit Sweden, Jason pulled the three-quarter pyramid out of storage. He longed for his old friend and its radiating sparkle. He missed it dearly but understood this phase of life was for family. Hopefully, he'd be able to pull it out later, when Peanut was a bit older.

As year turned into year, Jason began to understand the sacred role of relationships in healing. After all, he'd spent plenty of time clearing out the emotional debris from his past, long before he met Pia. However, intimate relationships like marriage, seemed to take healing up a notch.

Every time Jason and Pia got into an argument or fell into the blame and defend ritual, Jason noticed the encounters brought up old stuff from his past. On the surface it looked like a quarrel over money, household chores or childcare. But it never was, if he looked deeper. It was about manipulation, power or self-worth. Pia was just a prop in his personal drama, helping him experience his own crap. Whenever they argued, it was an opportunity to heal something. Sometimes he made the effort. Sometimes he didn't, which stuffed it away to emerge later (something it always did).

Living with Pia helped him understand an underlying principle about relationships. They're all mirrors. Jason was an accumulation of everyone he'd ever loved or hated. He had bits and pieces of everyone he'd ever met inside of himself. They created a response inside, shaping him into the person he was. That included the good, the bad and the ugly. If he didn't like something about someone, it brought up stuff he didn't like about himself. If he admired someone, it was part of himself he had yet to develop. Pia was no exception. In fact, she magnified the concept tenfold.

Jason loved her spirit of adventure, the fact she was from another country, and her love for the outdoors. She also chapped his ass over her insecurity with money, resistance to change, and bouts of emotional instability. She was an identical female version of him. That helped him discover a universal truth about relationships.

To find the perfect partner, you must be the perfect partner. Like attracts like. When someone engages in their own healing, they attract someone else who has healed, thereby improving the quality of the next relationship. It was imperative for Jason to do his own healing before meeting Pia. She had been doing hers too. As the two of them grew together, they helped each other. It was mutual growth and maturation through relationship.

And so it went for the next twelve years.

*

Vision - The Hindus
By this time, Jason was in his early forties. It was his third consecutive year working as a mineral exploration geologist. Corporate work certainly had its perks and excitement but more often than not, Jason found it to be a real drag. He was working four-weeks-on and four-weeks-off in remote locations like the Yukon and Brazil. He was frequently exhausted. Plus, it put a hefty burden on his relationship with Pia. However, the money was good and he had long stretches of time off to pursue his healing vocation.

During one of his breaks, Jason landed a paid volunteer position at the local hospital, providing healing services to cancer patients. Much to his surprise, much of his work was met with great success. However, the more he worked with subtle energies of the human aura, the more he felt like something was missing. There was another level he just couldn't get to. He knew there was something deeper...something larger.

It was God, or whatever else fits the description of a benevolent Creator. The more he read about spiritual awakenings, the more certain he was he'd never had one. Sure, he felt energy during his healing sessions. But those were just extensions of himself. There had to be something more. He desperately yearned for that connection and vowed he would do whatever necessary to make it happen.

A few days after making his personal vow, Jason had a night of very uneasy sleep. He tossed and turned for hours. He felt like some kind of uncontrollable electricity had been let loose in his body.

When he finally drifted off and the subconscious doors of dreamland were opened, Jason sensed a humanoid shape forming on the periphery of his awareness. The form was composed of an amorphous combination of light and liquid. Although, it remained stationary, the energy inside was constantly in motion. Jason stood and reveled in its highly energetic presence, for what seemed like hours. Eventually, the humanoid figure started to flicker, as it mysteriously displayed more distinctive features.

What came into focus was not one but two people. It appeared they were a sacred husband and wife from India. The man was dressed in a white robe with a golden stole draped about his neck. The woman wore an elaborate pastel sari. She also had a red dot painted in the middle of her forehead. Jason didn't know much about eastern religions but guessed they were Hindu.

They were seated with their eyes closed, side-by-side, in a posture of devotion with their hands gently touching in prayer. Eventually, they turned their hands outward and directed their palms at Jason, as if giving him an invisible blessing. The energy radiating off their hands nearly bowled him over. As the intensity continued to pour in, Jason thought he might explode and prayed they would stop. After several more moments of the electric barrage, the couple withdrew their energy and went back into prayer.

Jason was locked in an hypnotic gaze with both of their images as they slowly faded from view. When the Hindus disappeared completely, they were replaced by an enormous white temple, and then, a large golden ball. The three images, the couple, the temple and the ball, faded in and out of each other for an immeasurable amount of time and eventually dwindled back into an amorphous liquid-light shape.

Before they vanished completely, Jason was jolted awake, realizing he'd been visited by another spiritual guide.

Pia's Surprise
The last couple of years had taken its toll on Jason and Pia. Jason's long working stints were a strain on Pia, and as circumstances dictated, they were developing separate lives of their own. To bridge the gap, Jason phoned home regularly. However, he didn't exactly look forward to his evening calls to Pia. Instead of a ritual of reconnecting, Jason felt like it was a venue for Pia to complain. He knew her life was challenging when he was gone. Hell, he heard about it every time they spoke. But it seemed to be getting worse and he dreaded calling home.

Jason was in the middle of a 28-day shift, when he gave Pia a "hi-how-ya-doing" evening call. She was visiting relatives in Sweden with Peanut. Much to Jason's pleasant surprise, Pia was particularly upbeat. She was excited about something she'd discovered in Sweden. Confidently, she exclaimed, "It's a surprise you're going to love." He couldn't wait to get home and find out.

When Jason got home, he'd barely set his bags down when Pia broadcasted her latest revelation. "I've discovered meditation!" she proclaimed, overflowing with self-respect. "Someone in Sweden turned me on to a wonderful new school called Oneness University. I brought home an entire DVD introductory course." She proudly stretched out her arm and handed Jason the complete boxed set.

Jason couldn't believe Pia was bringing Oneness back around full circle. The small India-based meditation school, Jason had attended in Fiji, was now a full-scale university with three separate campuses. Since Jason took classes there, almost 15 years ago, global attendance exploded.

There was no doubt what Jason would be doing on his break. He was going back to school, à la DVD mini-course.

Guides - The Hindus
Oneness University had been founded by a husband and wife team from India. Jason took one look at them on the cover of the first DVD, and was immediately transported back to Chevron Mountain. They were the Hindu couple from his visions. Jason knew this signaled the next phase in his development. He desperately hoped it would lead him to a new triangle. However, he didn't know what phase of life he was supposed to be completing. At present, life seemed fairly stable and moving along in high gear. Plus, he never imagined a triangle would come through Pia. Their relationship was focused on the physical reality of raising a family and the emotional growth accompanying it. Jason never viewed it as spiritual.

Oneness University centered itself around a phenomenon that was in its infancy when Jason was in Fiji. It was called the Oneness Blessing. Apparently, it started with a small group of school children one day during recess. They were simply doing what kids do, playing with a ball. However, this was no ordinary ball. It was an energetic ball of golden light, created by the imagination. The children soon discovered they could pass the ball back and forth, from inside themselves to the inside of other kids. All it took was a touch of the hands. It was a delightful form of imaginary entertainment. However, it didn't take long for adults to witness miracles surrounding the children's fun. There were physical healings, a reduction in all types of emotional duress, and a significant increase in scholastic achievement. The kids had clearly stumbled onto something important.

The Hindu couple who ran the school immediately recognized the golden ball for what it was, namely Divine energy. It didn't take long to develop the blessing into courses for adults. By the time Jason reunited with Oneness for the second time, it was a global sensation. Over one million Indian nationals, and thousands of others from all over the world, had been through their programs. Oneness blossomed into a world-wide experiential university, based on awakening to Divine presence. Thanks to Pia, Jason's prayers were answered.

In theory, it worked like this: By laying hands on the head of a recipient, an awakened practitioner generated a blessing of energy. That energy then created a neurobiological shift in brain chemistry, permanently opening pathways to connect to Divine presence. Once a recipient was awakened through a training program, they were then qualified to help others awaken with the blessing.

When Jason first learned of the blessing, he crossed his arms and said to himself, "I dunno. That's way too simple. Looks like the stuff of cults, if you ask me." But after he finished the DVD course, he researched more about the University. Jason grew to appreciate their commitment to a positive vision of the future. In a world entrenched in negativity, teetering on the brink of destruction, he thought Oneness University might be worth looking into. Plus, Anandaji had been promoted to lead Dasa (teacher) and was running programs all over southern India. When Jason discovered that little pearl of info, he was all for it.

*

Pia soon discovered a trained practitioner who gave blessings once a week, at the local community center. Within a few weeks she became a devout follower, receiving blessings every chance she could. Jason tagged along when he wasn't working. But quite honestly, he didn't feel a thing. Pia, on the other hand, was quite clearly affected. Jason couldn't put his finger on it but there was some kind of subtle shift happening in her. When he pointed it out, she didn't seem to recognize it in herself. However, Jason sensed a gap growing between them. He also noticed, she seemed to be spending a lot of time on the Internet.

After about a month of blessings, Pia made arrangements to take a one-week course in Fiji, just like Jason had over a decade ago. When she returned, she was ecstatic. She had been turned on to a wonderful new dimension she'd never known before. She was so enraptured, Jason thought she'd had an affair with Oneness University itself. He didn't want to admit it, but he was totally jealous. He wanted to be excited like that too.

Soon after Pia's return, Jason departed for his next work assignment. This one was in Nunavut, Canada, about 125 southwest of the Arctic Ocean's Bathurst Inlet. It was like working on Mars. The word remote didn't come close to describing the desolation of the Canadian Barren Lands. Jason felt more distant from his family than ever before. It seemed the isolation in the wilderness somehow reflected his relationship with Pia.

However, her state of exuberance continued long after Jason left for the boonies. She was so upbeat during their evening calls, she scarcely inquired about Jason or his work. It was all Oneness this and Oneness that. Jason mostly bit his tongue, nodded, smiled and kicked himself for being jealous about her spiritual awakening.

About two months later, when Jason returned from one of his 28-day working stints, Pia became increasingly distant. Her conversations were curt, she rarely made eye contact, and she walked out whenever Jason entered the room. Furthermore, she was brash, forward and annoyingly overconfident. Jason knew she was heading into her mid-life crisis years. He also knew that whatever was bubbling up inside of her was aggressively assisted by the Oneness Blessings.

Meanwhile, the blessings continued.

A few weeks later, Pia decided to return to Oneness University and take the second-level course, held in India. Jason had a break in his schedule at that time and thought he'd go too. It would be a wonderful opportunity to reconcile the distance between them. When he ran the idea by Pia, she became irate, like he was crashing her party. When Jason asserted himself and said he was going anyway, Pia antagonistically replied, "Well, okay but we're going to travel as 'just friends.'"

Jason couldn't believe his ears. "Huh? What the hell is that supposed to mean?" Pia didn't respond. In total frustration, Jason clenched his teeth and said, "Okay..Fine...Whatever."

That did it. Pia had crossed the line. She'd gone from distant and obscure to flat-out weird. He couldn't believe some of the garbage coming out of her mouth. They'd been inseparable for almost 12 years and suddenly, Jason had no idea who she was. In a matter of weeks, Pia had morphed into a completely different person. Whatever was happening, one thing was clear to Jason: those Oneness Blessings were a force to be reckoned with.

Chapter 7
Awakening

Oneness Again

It seemed like forever, but they finally arrived in India. Pia and Jason traveled over 36 hours and never spoke, mainly, because Pia arranged seats on opposite ends of the airplane. When they arrived at Oneness University, they were separated again. Unknown to Jason, Pia registered for the course scheduled for Northern Europeans. He was signed up for the American and Canadian course. They would be on different campuses the entire week. Jason was completely pissed off and dumbfounded by her deceit. All he could think was, "What is up with her? Why is she being so sneaky?"

Jason congregated with the group of 30 he'd be spending the week with. They were no slouches. Everyone had taken at least one previous course through the University. Furthermore, each person had been individually screened by staff administrators. There was an American representative from the Dali Lama, a Catholic cardinal, a Hollywood director and producer, a professional football coach, a self-help celebrity, a well-known model, a leading cancer research physician, and a host of other "normal" people like Jason. It took Jason two full days to adjust to the company he was keeping.

In addition, his assigned roommate, Dr. Greg Anderson, was a phenomenal naturopathic doctor from Canada who cured himself from environmental poisoning, using methods he'd invented. In his younger days, he also played on the Canadian Olympic basketball team. Together, he and Jason would be mutual springboards, assisting each other in a week of remarkable spiritual growth.

The class structure was similar to the courses in Fiji. It began with morning stretching and meditation, followed by teaching and contemplation in the afternoon. However, the evening meditations were now enhanced with the Oneness Blessing, given inside the University's temple.

The blessing givers were some of the strangest people Jason had ever seen. They dressed in white and had shaven heads. Plus, they never interacted with any of the students and Jason never saw them speak. Most of them were very reclusive and had difficulty functioning in the regular physical world. They seemed like aliens from another universe—supreme conduits of energy, consumed with Divine presence. As much as Jason wanted to evolve in his spirituality, he certainly didn't want to end up like them. He enjoyed hiking too much.

The Temple
The Oneness temple was about fives miles from Jason's campus, surrounded by the third-world agricultural landscape of southeastern India. It was enormous and reminded Jason of the Taj Mahal. Built of white marble, it was a visual spectacle for the entire region. People came from miles around just to be in its presence.

The temple was designed to be a continuously radiating beacon of Divine energy. It was loaded with sacred geometry and intentional energetic motifs to maximize Divine presence. In the center of the temple on the second floor, was a large open circular room, with eight evenly spaced arched doorways. Each entrance represented a specific human virtue, assisting in Divine connection. In the middle of the room was a golden ball, symbolizing the Oneness Blessing. No one was allowed in the room except blessing givers. They were in continual states of deep meditation, ensuring constant interaction with the Divine.

Each evening, groups of up to 30, from three different campuses, were guided through parts of the temple. They were assembled based on nationality, such as Canadian/American, Northern European and Eastern Asia. There were at least seven different groups touring the temple when Jason was there.

Across the magnificent corridor, Jason saw the Northern European group, featuring the one and only Pia. She was engrossed in conversation with some guy. Jason guessed she saw him too but never once looked in his direction. As Jason's group passed Pia's, she refused to look up and make eye contact. "Weird," he thought, as he tried to shrug it off. "I give up."

As stragglers in the Northern European group passed, Jason locked eyes with a woman who was about 15 years his senior. Their gaze remained curiously fixed on each other as they passed. They politely smiled. It was obvious both of them recognized each other but neither of them knew from where.

After the tour, Jason's group was led into a meditation room. Everyone was seated on the floor, lights were dimmed, and soft music played. They were ready for their first blessing from a human conduit. Each person stood and filed into line when their turn came around. During the blessing a few people shrieked, one lady passed out completely, and a couple of people strongly convulsed. Jason, on the other hand, didn't feel a thing. As he disappointedly returned to his seat, a light flashed in his head. "Ula!" The woman he passed in the corridor was Ula, his royal Dutch friend from Findhorn!

Awakening Activations
That night in his dreams, Jason found himself at a conference table. Sitting in the chairs were some of the more prominent students in the class. They were Divine power brokers, archetypes from Jason's subconscious. Each one of them contained an undiscovered aspect of his psyche, sub-personalities yet to be developed.

The next morning, Jason woke up a little dizzy. It seemed like the entire cosmos had changed overnight. There was a plasmatic, surreal quality to everything. He thought if he poked his finger into the air, ripples would be cast off in all directions. Reality had taken on the consistency of half-set jello—malleable, pliable, and not completely physical. When Jason walked into the morning meditation room, he saw the people from his dream. He wondered if they were actually real or some kind of subconscious projection. A little disoriented, he thought, "My, that blessing sure did something."

The morning meditation led to an experience of the Divine. Jason was feeling strange to begin with and drifted into very deep state of relaxation. Within minutes, the Hindu couple who founded Oneness University presented themselves. Jason felt he was being visited by God himself. Then it dawned on him that was exactly what was happening. As he squirmed in awe, the image of the Hindus shot into his body like a guided missile. Jerking, coughing and gasping for air, Jason let out a scream of panic.

Welcome to Oneness University. Awakening, part one.

The next day, at the evening blessing, Jason was waiting his turn like everyone else. His mind was wandering aimlessly when a humorous memory drifted through. He quietly gave a little chuckle. Then another. And another. Before he knew it, he broke into uproarious laughter. Furthermore, the laughter was contagious. Everyone was exploding into hysterics. It was like an incredible stand-up comedy show. Jason laughed so hard, tears started rolling and he peed his pants. It took every ounce of self-control to pull himself together.

The deep belly laughter opened Jason's psyche to a new level of feeling. The God of laughter had primed him for another blessing. After he received his hands-on, he laid down to collect himself. Uncontrollably, he rolled over on all fours and started to rock from head to front. He couldn't stop. At the same time, the circumference of his head felt an unbelievable restricting force. He thought it was going to crush his skull. Simultaneously, it felt like his entire body was being forced through a tight tube. The pain was intense, especially around his temples. Within moments, he pushed through the tube, as a brilliant light exploded through the top of his head. There to greet him was the Hindu couple of Oneness.

Instead of a warm and loving embrace, they summoned a tsunami of electrical energy. The wave picked them up and hurled them toward Jason, smashing into him like wrecking ball. He convulsed on the floor for a few minutes, then laid motionless for quite some time. Darkness ensued. Later that evening, he didn't remember how he got back to his room.

Oneness strikes again. Awakening, part two.

That night, Jason was trying to sort out his experience and asked Dr. Greg what he thought had happened. Greg said, "I've read about similar spiritual episodes with Aboriginal clans in Australia, during their walkabouts. It sounds like you had a Rebirthing experience. It can happen at the beginning of a major life transformation."

"Makes sense, I guess," Jason said. "It sure felt like being born. Do you think I'll be going through a big change?"

"Well, if you do," Dr. Greg said, "I hope I don't have to go to the Australian outback to do it."

*

Each day they watched recorded video teachings, covering a wide array of topics. Anandaji gave most of the presentations. Jason hoped to see him again. However, Anandaji was very busy and traveled frequently. Seeing him didn't seem too likely. For Jason, that was a shame because as spectacular as the videos were, it was a poor substitute for visiting his old friend in person.

After lunch that day, Jason wandered to the far end of the walled campus to stroll through a sizable orange grove. With the amount of energy and information he was getting exposed to, it was imperative to have some alone time to process.

Walking along the 8-foot wall in the most remote corner, Jason thought he heard someone call his name. Caught off guard, he turned around but didn't see anyone. "That was weird," he thought, and kept walking. After a few more steps, he heard it again, only this time loud and clear. Now, he was clearly spooked. Nobody was there. "Okay," he thought, "I'm going crazy. This course in becoming too much for me." Then he closed his eyes to get a grip. That's when he saw him, plain as day. It was Anandaji, sitting in Jason's imagination. He shook his head hard in disbelief, trying to clear Anandaji's image. But it wouldn't go away. Jason was sure he was going out of his mind. He felt like he needed medication instead of meditation.

Anandaji transported himself from Jason's imagination and walked along side of him. The only problem was he wasn't physical. He was a projected, life-size image, from Jason's subconscious. Ambling along, they carried on a conversation that lasted at least thirty minutes. The conversation was very explicit, teaching Jason about surrendering to Divine presence, without losing himself in the process. Anandaji told stories, gave examples, and did some simple demonstrations.

Jason was captivated but that didn't change the fact he thought he was going mad.

As they came to the end of the grove, Anandaji stood aside and grinned a mischievous smile. He knew something Jason didn't. Suddenly, a man and a woman appeared in the tree above. It was the Hindu founders of Oneness. Jason couldn't believe his eyes. He knew this encounter wasn't tangible, at least not in the physical sense. However, the events were so lucid it was impossible to determine what was real and what wasn't.

Anandaji giggled with delight, as the couple drifted down from the tree. Centering themselves in front of Jason, they said with the most endearing of smiles, "Remember Jason, it's all about letting go. You need to learn how to surrender to Divine Will." Without another word the bearded man placed his hands on Jason head, while the woman gently placed her hands over his heart. "There…very good…that's it," they gently encouraged.

Jason closed his eyes and absorbed their energy to his core. It was as powerful as it was gentle. It felt like his entire body was melting. After a few moments, he gently re-opened his eyes to revel in their presence. But as he squinted, the couple slowly spun in a few circles and dissolved into his body. Surprised and confused, Jason looked over to Anandaji for some kind of explanation. Anandaji was gone. Suddenly, Jason was alone.

Oneness again. Awakening, part three.

Triangle Four
The last day of the retreat was Jason's birthday. In the morning, he was scheduled for a 15-minute meeting with one of the instructors, for any remaining questions. However, after all he'd been through, he thought about skipping it. A one-on-one meeting felt like too much work. He kicked the idea around through breakfast and finally decided to go. When Jason arrived, he knocked on the door and heard a soft-spoken, "Come in." Much to his jaw-dropping surprise, it was Anandaji, this time in flesh and blood. It had been over a decade since he'd last seen him. Anandaji hadn't aged a day.

Anandaji didn't say a word. When Jason sat down, he locked his glazed-over eyes onto Jason's and entered a very deep trance. Within moments, Jason felt waves of buzzing energy, radiating from Anandaji's eyes into his own. Jason couldn't move. He didn't know what was happening but it felt like his entire chakra system was being blown wide open. Whatever the case, Anandaji was intent on completing the process. He kept at it for another two hours.

Awakening complete. Oneness, part four.

When Anandaji completed his energy transmission, he held up his palms about heart high. With a gaze that could bend metal, he focused with all his might. Slowly, a cloud of swirling golden light emerged, just above his hands. Jason shuddered. As the vortex continued to spin, a physical object appeared in its center. Unbelievably, it was another golden triangle. When it became fully physical, Anandaji gently plucked it out of the air. Very amused with himself, he laughed and said, "I believe this belongs to you." Then he handed it to Jason.

After Jason took the triangle, Anandaji touched his hands in prayer, beamed an enormous grin, and bowed his head. Before Jason could react, Anandaji stood up, touched Jason lightly on the shoulder and said, "We're not done yet my friend." Without another word, he spun light as a feather, and slipped out the door.

Ula Returns
After the course was over, all of the participants from the three campuses congregated at the bus departure zone. It was a typical Indian madhouse. Jason wondered how a country, steeped in the mystical, couldn't get its act together on some of the most basic elements of life, like loading buses and indoor plumbing.

As he tried to make his way through the morass of confusion, Jason spotted Ula waiting to board her bus. Enthusiastically, they both recognized each other and greeted with an impassioned, heartfelt embrace. However, there was too much to say, too much ground to cover, in the midst of all the mayhem.

Ula told Jason she'd be spending the better part of the following week visiting an ashram in a town called Pondicherry. Jason's plan was to spend the next few days with Pia, not far from there, in Mahabalipuram, visiting ancient temples carved from stone. However, the idea of being with Pia made Jason exceedingly nervous. He had no idea what was going on in her twisted mind. After an incredible week, spending time with her was the last thing he wanted to do. He had the sneaking suspicion that whatever she might say would make him sick to his stomach. That could wait until he got home. So Ula and Jason set a time, day and location to meet in Pondicherry.

Shortly after talking with Ula, Pia and Jason made their way to Mahabalipuram, via bus and taxi. They hadn't spoken to each other in over a week. The silent, awkward time together in the taxi nearly brought Jason to tears. He had absolutely no clue why she wouldn't talk to him.

Eventually, they arrived at their hotel and booked a room with separate beds. Jason was severely stressed and didn't know what to do, so he visited the temples and kept walking, long into the night. At sunrise the next morning, while Pia was still sleeping, he was up and off to visit Ula.

Ula and Jason met in a cafe on the edge of the French Quarter in Pondicherry. It was an interesting part of town. Simply by crossing the street, you were transported from India to the sidewalks of France. The streets in the French Quarter were un-customarily spotless and named in French, creating a French oasis in the midst of third-world India. Ula's ashram was centered there.

The Unity Council
They met at noon. By three in the afternoon, they were still chatting away, filling each other in on every nuance of their lives since Findhorn. When the conversation finally died down, Ula looked at Jason with the utmost sincerity and said, "Jason, I didn't come to India for an elaborate spiritual vacation. I'm here on a very specific mission." Jason straightened up, as the conversation shifted into a more serious mood.

"You may not remember this," she said, "but when we were in Findhorn, you said something that changed my life forever."

"I did?" Jason mumbled wide-eyed, like he'd done something wrong.

"In a way, you saved my life. I'd been in Findhorn for a couple of years, essentially hiding out and feeling sorry for myself. You came along and said: 'Everybody suffers. The question is, what are you going to do about it?' Do you remember that?"

Jason emphatically shook his head in a gesture of absolute denial.

"That comment hit a major nerve. I never forgot it. In fact, it lit a fire under my butt that has been burning ever since. It set me on a spiritual revolution.

"A typical conversation around Findhorn in those days was that humanity was on the verge of a spiritual transformation. I heard it a lot and had plenty of time to think about it. Then you came along and woke me up. I thought, okay then, how does a global shift in consciousness happen? Through action...and Divine Will, of course. Then I thought some more.

"I thought of my blessings. I was lucky enough, being born into excessive wealth. That arena has offered me access to some of the most influential and affluent people on the planet. I decided it was time to stop bemoaning my fate and use those connections to help further the evolution of humanity. Shortly after you left Findhorn, I came up with the idea of the Unity Council. I've put my heart and soul into it ever since.

"I wondered, 'What would be the most effective way to enhance spirituality across the entire planet?' I knew there were institutions already in place, set on accomplishing that, such as the Findhorn Foundation and Oneness University. Then I wondered if it was possible to give those institutions, and humanity in general, a spiritual boost.

"It seemed to me, that it could be done by gathering the right people on a regular basis, to transmit spiritual energy into the world. In a way, the idea was similar to Oneness University. However, instead of using a golden ball, we'd be using people.

"Over the past decade, that's what we've been able to do. You'd be amazed at the level of support and interest we've been able to generate. We have successful members from all walks of life and every corner of the globe. We've tried to represent nearly every facet of society.

"However, we had several conditions for invitees to the Council. First, they had to be actively involved in their own spiritual practice, on a very high level. Second, they needed to be in positions that could reach a significant amount of people. Third, they couldn't be in the media spotlight. That meant we wanted people with a high level of spirituality and influence but a relatively low level of visibility. We weren't trying to create a secret society but we certainly wanted to keep things quiet. The last thing we wanted to do was create a venue for powerfully insecure people to bolster their egos. We had problems with a couple of people like that in the beginning. However, the energies we were activating were too strong for that kind of nonsense. Unfortunately, they more or less self-destructed. Both were American men.

"The Council is currently comprised of about 30 people from all over the world. It's roughly a 50/50 mix of men and women. But it's not a constant or fixed number. It's continually changing. The reason I came to Oneness University, besides going through their program, was to connect with some faculty from the University. There were also select individuals attending the course that I wanted to meet in person. Two of them were in your group.

"The premise of the Council is quite simple. We meet three of four times a year at a select retreat location. Based on information we are able to receive from a higher intelligence, we set a theme for the retreat. Then the action begins. Over the course of three days, the entire group opens itself to Divine energy downloads. When the retreat is over, everyone simply returns to their normal lives and silently radiates energy to everyone they come in contact with. It's an undercover White Op campaign. No evangelizing, no politicizing, no fund raising.

"Success of the Council has been phenomenal, in specific projects and programs. Everything from technological breakthroughs, to lasting brokered peace deals, to enduring financial stability, to unbelievable environmental repair. It would take a book to list the miracles. However, we still haven't reached our goal of a worldwide spiritual transformation. We're missing a few crucial pieces to the puzzle and we don't know what they are."

When Ula finished talking, Jason sat in silence for quite some time. After careful deliberation, he eventually looked Ula straight in the eye and said, "I think I have something to tell you…On second thought…I think I have something to show you."

Jason cautiously untucked his shirt, pulled it up, and unzipped the money belt he was carrying around his waist. Slowly and carefully, he pulled out the triangle Anandaji had given him only two days before.

Ula gasped. After the initial shock wore off, they both studied it in fascination. It seemed like gold but clearly not fashioned by human hands. Unlike the other triangles, it was nearly translucent with a bizarre electric-plastic quality. On the back were 21 unknown symbols, like the others. On the front was a triangle with a human eye, like the pyramid on the back of an American one-dollar bill. While they were studying it, they thought they saw the eye blink a couple of times. Ula could also feel it buzz in her hands, as if it were trying to communicate something to her.

Jason spent the next half-hour filling Ula in on the details of the three-quarter pyramid he had in storage. Ula listened intently until he finished. Then, she gently but assertively said, "You know Jason, you and the triangles are all a part of this. We've been reunited for a reason."

Jason nervously tipped back in his chair and crossed his arms. In mild regret, he proceeded to squench his lips to one side and said, "Yeah, I 'spose so."

Ula tenderly lifted her hand, touching Jason's cheek and said, "My dear courageous boy. Wherever you are headed in this life, your darling Pia may not be able to go. Please, try not to hold on too tight."

Jason's heart sank like a brick and tears welled up in his eyes. He paused for a moment as he looked down, then reluctantly nodded his head, whispering a very raspy, "Okay."

It was getting dark and there was no way Jason was going to make it back to Pia that night. That was fine with him because he was starting to dread the inevitable. Ula had an extra room in her flat and offered it to him for the night. Jason politely accepted. She further perked his curiosity by saying, "There's someone I'd like you to meet."

Hakeem

It was about six blocks from the cafe to Ula's flat. When she opened the door, she joyfully chimed out, "Yoo-hoo! I'm home."

A gentleman sitting on the veranda immediately rose and gave Ula a loving hug.

"Jason, this is my partner Hakeem. Hakeem, this is Jason. He's the one I've told you so much about."

"Ahhh...," Hakeem said, tilting is head back in acknowledgement. He politely extended his hand and greeted, "I'm honored to make your acquaintance."

Jason felt exceedingly self-conscious, like a mere mortal shaking hands with a Greek God. "Likewise," he replied, then thought, "Likewise? Wow, that sounds pretty stupid...And did he say honored? To meet me? Doesn't he know I get dirt under my fingernails when I work?"

From one look at Hakeem, Jason could see he ran in social circles several stratospheres above him. The word elite didn't quite stretch high enough. Hakeem looked like some Arabian prince or other. After all, that made sense if he was hooked up with Ula. Jason later found out he came from one of the wealthiest families in Saudi Arabia.

Hakeem was one of the most handsome specimens Jason had ever laid eyes on. He was tall and lean, immaculately groomed, and decked out in very expensive clothing. His neatly trimmed black hair and beard beautifully offset his unblemished olive skin. His perfect, dazzling white smile was the kind saved by God exclusively for Arab men. The finishing touch to his god-like aura was a faint hint of cologne that wafted around him like a celestial presence. He was educated, suave, sophisticated, gentle, gracious, kind, charming and completely unpretentious. But most striking to Jason was how visibly he loved Ula. He made no attempt to hide it. They absolutely sparkled in each other's company.

Ula went on to say, "Tomorrow I'm meeting some people in a place called Auroville to discuss the Unity Council. I was hoping you and Hakeem would come along and tour the grounds while I'm in my meeting. I think you'll really like it."

Hakeem and Jason looked at each other and nodded in agreement.

"Great," she said, "Tomorrow it's off to Auroville."

In spite of disturbing thoughts about Pia, Jason slept very well that night. He knew the hand of the Divine he'd felt so strongly at Oneness University was still with him.

Auroville
Jason had never heard of Auroville. He was fascinated to discover it was similar in size to Oneness University. The brochure said, "Auroville is meant to be a universal town where men and women of all countries can live in peace and progressive harmony, above all creeds, all politics and all nationalities. The purpose of Auroville is to realize human unity." Like Oneness University, Auroville was also centered around a golden ball. However, the ball in the temple at Oneness University was about three feet across. The golden ball at Auroville, called the Matrimandir, was about six stories high. It was designed as "a place to find one's consciousness."

When Hakeem and Jason arrived for a tour, the office to the public was closed for the day. Tours were not available. So they took a self-guided expedition on a path around the Matrimandir's gated perimeter.

When they arrived at the overview area, Jason could feel energy coming off the ball, from over 100 meters away. The energy grew so strong, he could actually see it. It looked like rolling ocean waves. Before Jason knew what was happening, the energy penetrated the ground, causing a commotion like an earthquake. He glanced at Hakeem, whose eyes were widened in panic. Strangely enough, no one else around them seemed to notice a thing. When the final wave of energetic motion rolled by, it was replaced by a feeling of remarkable serenity. It stayed with Jason and Hakeem on their walk throughout the village. By evening, remnants of the sensation still remained. Such was Auroville.

On their walk back to the community center, Hakeem explained to Jason, "Auroville and Oneness University lie on heighten areas of Earth energy, called transecting ley lines. They've been built in their precise locations with highly conscious intent, making this part of the planet an energy lighthouse for Divine presence. The combination of intensified Earth energy, human intention, and action, allows the miraculous to become commonplace. This region is ideal for personal transformation. Ula and I want to be involved, to assist this area in the next revolutionary step: collective global transformation."

*

When the taxi pulled up to Ula's flat to take Jason back to Mahabalipuram, Hakeem extended a gracious embrace and Ula smacked a kiss on his cheek. Then, she took a step back and announced, "I'll be seeing you soon. I'd love to see the rest of your triangles. I'll be in touch."

As Jason rode back to Mahabalipuram, he was overwhelmed with gratitude for his miraculous visit to SE India. He knew his life had been changed forever. However, he had a gnawing, anxious feeling in his gut. He wasn't too excited to see it play out back home.

Pia's Pronouncement
Jason nervously fumbled with his keys, as he unlocked the door to the hotel room. Pia was there, packing her bags, and looked up at Jason with complete indifference. Passively, she snorted, "Oh, it's you. Better get packed, we need to get moving to the airport."

It was another silent taxi ride, followed by a day-and-a-half flight back home, on opposite ends of the airplane. Jason's stomach was still trembling. He wasn't sure how the scenario with Pia was going to roll out, but from his angle, it didn't look good.

Three days later, when the oblivious Jason walked into the living room, Pia reached her wits end. She was absolutely annoyed with a man who was constantly walking on eggshells. Finally, she confronted him and spat, "I want out."

Jason, in complete ignorance, replied, "Out of what?"

With knives in her eyes, she looked at him with intolerable irritation and wondered how someone could be so stupid. "Our marriage, you idiot. I want a divorce."

Jason's walls of denial immediately started to crumble. "Why?" he pleaded in a panicked and perplexed rage. Pia didn't respond. "Fine!" he screamed, then turned and slammed the door on his exit. Within minutes, he was on the Internet, filing out forms for divorce.

A few weeks later, Jason's life had completely imploded. He was living alone in a one-room basement apartment wondering how the hell he got there. After he thought about for a while, he figured it was simple enough. Oneness University had facilitated an enormous inner change. Now, it was revealing itself in his outer world. Unfortunately, the result of his awakening required him let go of his former life completely. Heartbroken, he frequently thought, "If this is what spiritual growth is all about, then to hell with it. It's too damn devastating."

However, at the same time, an incredible spiritual energy he'd never felt before became permanently active. He could feel his chakras spinning all the time. A buzz of energy constantly emanated from his hands and feet. More often than not, he felt like a walking light socket. His experiences at Oneness University stripped away something, exposing a quantum leap of internal energy. He was no longer the same person.

For the next two years, life for Jason was an enormous, razor-sharp, two-edged sword of a roller coaster ride. On one hand, he'd been irreversibly opened to mystical spirituality. On the other hand, he was caught in the tidal waves of grief from an unwanted divorce. There was more than one day he lay in bed until noon with the covers pulled over his head. His only friends were the shards of glass forming the shattered remnants of his heart. He became increasingly distraught. In desperation, he went to see a fortuneteller. Maybe a glimpse into his future would give him a little peace of mind.

The Reading
It was only two weeks since he'd split from Pia when he scheduled his psychic reading. The woman conducting the reading was a fairly well respected Tarot card reader in town. When Jason entered her office, he was exceedingly self-conscious, emotionally frail, and teetering on the edge of hopelessness.

As the cards flipped out, one after the other, the medium sank into a trance. The timbre and cadence of her voice altered, as she prepared to channel her guides. About half way into the reading, she turned over a card called the Lovers. Her eyes twinkled as she grasped her heart and dreamily sighed, "There's love coming into your life…and it appears to be very soon."

"No!" Jason screamed in defiance. He yelled so loud, it snapped the fortuneteller out her trance and scared the living bejeezus out of her. She instinctively recoiled and lifted her hands in self-defense. Cowering in the chair, she feared Jason was going to take a swing at her. Innocently, she snapped back, "Hey, I'm just trying to relay information from my guides. Don't get mad."

With 30 minutes still on the clock, Jason stood up and said, "Screw it," then promptly walked out the door. As soon as he made it to the sidewalk, he bent over at the waist and wept. "No, no, no, no, no! I can't do it. I'm not ready."

In that state of distress, Jason went to his storage unit and recovered the three-quarter pyramid. It had been sitting silently for over a decade. He desperately wanted to feel better. He figured if he could fit the triangle Anandaji had given him, it would give off magical energy to heal his broken heart. So he sped like a madman to retrieve it.

Jason arrived home in a state of aggravation and rushed into his apartment. He grabbed the triangle, lying on the nightstand next to his bed. Without taking pause for even a breath, he held the triangle up to the three-quarter pyramid, with shaking hands. Nothing happened. It didn't fit. The size and shape were okay but there were indentations on the sides instead of tabs. Desperately, he kept jamming it into place, begging it to go in. But it wouldn't take. In absolute defeat, like a dagger had just ripped through his heart, Jason flopped facedown on his bed and cried... and cried...and cried.

The Hospital
During his dark days of grief, Jason had one major blessing going for him. It was his work at the hospital. It didn't take him long to discover he could channel his new-found spiritual energy through his hands. Quickly, he'd evolved into a full-blown spiritual healer. Miracles were happening in his sessions. A number of patients went into full remission, a few spontaneously. The healing didn't stop with cancer either. He healed issues around family, fear of

dying, depression, eating disorders, relationship problems, compulsive disorders, and anxiety attacks. The list went on and on. There were many days he found it hard to believe the successes his clients were telling him.

However, as often as he played the role of the healer, he was called to played the role of the priest. For every patient who went into remission, he prepared just as many for a peaceful death. In those cases, he was an instrument of Divine will, helping people cross over to the other side. It was awkward for him initially. However, he soon discovered how beautiful it was. It was a sacred position, reserved for the moment of ultimate transition. As time went by, he felt honored to do it, far more than he could ever express.

Chapter 8
Union

Guide - Madonna One

Despite all the miracles at the hospital, when Jason returned home, his grief was always there waiting. In fact, his grief loved their quality time alone together. And if evenings together weren't enough, the two of them took it up a notch on weekends. It was the time of week Jason dreaded the most, long hours alone with his grief.

One weekend, a married couple Jason knew in passing, Dale and Sylvie, invited him on a backpacking trip. They knew he was going through a tough stretch and figured a little outing into the wilderness might do him some good. Jason eagerly accepted. He was packed and ready to go, three days ahead of time.

It wasn't a long hike, only about eight miles up an alpine glacial valley. At five miles, the old-growth rainforest gave way to ankle-high vegetation, made up of heather and willow. At six miles, they had to cross a stream through freezing glacial melt water. That was where the trail ended for the majority of day hikers. On the other side of the stream, the poorly maintained trail continued up the valley. However, it was so sketchy, they lost it completely in a few spots. At seven miles, the valley was abruptly truncated by a 30-foot vertical cliff. There, the stream shot off the ledge, creating a magnificent rainbow-hued waterfall. However, the only way to continue up the valley was straight up and over the cliff, using climbing ropes.

To mountaineers, it was an easy climb. Plenty of permanent hardware was in the cliff face, left by previous climbers. So up they went. In no time flat, the three of them were alone, in a sheer, dead-end, box-canyon wilderness, appropriately named Paradise Valley. The beauty was breathtaking. The valley floor was matted with velvety green foliage and mystifying waterfalls sprayed 1,000 feet, over bluish-gray vertical cliffs.

They continued another mile, up to the end of the valley and made camp. It was the last suitable spot to pitch tents. A hundred yards or so past their campsite, the canyon made a right hand turn. That was essentially the end of the flat part of the valley floor. From there, the heather slope steepened until it met boulders and talus that tumbled off the canyon walls. Surrounded by cliffs on three sides, the only way out of the valley was back the way they had come.

It was late afternoon when Jason finished putting up his tent. He was knackered from both the hike and the weight of grief he carried in his heart. The saving grace of the hike was that it distracted him from the abyss of sadness he felt in his chest. Trying not to think about anything, he crawled into his tent to catch a few winks before dinner.

As soon as his head hit the pillow, an enormous wave of grief welled up from the depths of his heart and engulfed his entire body. He was literally paralyzed. It felt like a full-bodied straight jacket, made from misery and wet cement. Forcing himself to focus on the moment, Jason observed the incredible sadness in great detached detail. It wasn't all from his divorce. This grief ran so deep, it was woven into the fabric of his being. He had no idea where it came from. It seemed like a universal loss, like the original separation from the Creator.

As soon as he connected that dot, the grief started to move. It felt like a giant rotating galaxy. Slowly…slowly…it turned and gently lifted up and out of his body. Then, as if it never existed, it dissolved and dissipated into the endless expanse of the Universe.

Jason slowly sat up. He felt like he'd just run a marathon. Attentively, he shifted his focus inward and took a quick emotional inventory. The weight he'd been carrying around his heart was gone. However, he wasn't overjoyed because it was more of an overwhelming relief. A relief earned through extensive and deliberate exertion.

Jason clambered out of his tent and noticed the sun had sunk behind the cliff face. Dale and Sylvie had fired up the stove and were cooking supper. They were also smoking pot. Jason was completely baffled as to why people, surrounded by such incredible beauty, would want to dull their senses. Shrugging his shoulders, he pulled up a rock and completed the circle around the stove. He tried to ignore what just happened in his tent and joined the sacred dinnertime ritual, filling the air with wilderness stories, while scarfing down piping hot soup.

As they chatter-boxed away in the dwindling daylight, they heard a sound from down the trail. All attentive, they turned their heads, expecting to encounter some kind of wildlife. What they saw was a four legged animal loping up the trail. It was a dog with a collar. "What the...?" Dale squawked in amazement. "How the hell did a dog get up here?" Trailing the dog, was a couple that looked to be in their 30s. Tagging along behind them was a robust teeny bop girl. Jason, Dale and Sylvie stared at each other in disbelief.

At first glance, nothing about them made sense. No one was carrying a backpack or any climbing gear. Second, they looked like models straight out of an outdoor fashion magazine. They weren't sweaty or dirty at all. Jason thought, "I'm sorry, but if you hike eight miles up a glacial valley, ford an ice-cold mountain stream, and scale a 30-foot vertical cliff, a little dirt and sweat are going to show. And what about the dog? Did they just toss him up the 30-foot cliff? What's the deal? Were they dropped from a spaceship? Something's fishy." As the four of them approached, the more Jason observed, the more they didn't seem right. Furthermore, Jason noticed the woman looked strangely familiar.

They were a delightful family from Sweden, traveling the US and Canada on holiday. The dog belonged to a friend of theirs in town. The kid was of their own making.

It was a friendly encounter, light and pleasant. But as the conversation carried on, Jason couldn't help but think about his former family, with a woeful feeling of longing.

Eventually, the trail took command of the situation and the Swedish family turned and continued their trek to the end of the valley. When they were about 100 feet away, Jason noticed something dropped from the back pocket of the woman. It looked like a map. He trotted up the trail, picked up the map, and called out to the young mother who was trailing well behind the others. "Excuse me, I think you dropped this."

She turned around, checked her back pocket, and with a grin walked back to Jason. He handed her the map. With an angelic sparkle in her eye, she winked and said, "Remember, we are always there for you." Without another word, she turned and jogged to catch up with her family.

Jason was staggered. It was the first Madonna from his vision triggered by Anandaji's handshake, so long ago in Fiji. He stood there with his mouth open and stared until they turned the corner. Shocked, he turned around and slowly ambled back to Dale and Sylvie. They had the hash pipe out again and offered Jason a hit but he declined. He just sat down on his rock and thought.

Jason knew it wasn't long until sunset. He also knew the Madonna and her family had to come back this way. Their gear was probably dropped at the base of the 30-foot cliff. They'd have to get back before dark.

As Jason sat in silence, ignoring Dale and Sylvie, his mind was flooded with memories of his visions. "Yes, yes...," he reminisced. "The vertical canyons...the waterfalls...the Madonnas. The Swedish woman's face seemed identical. But weren't there two Madonnas in the original vision on Chevron Mountain?"

Jason could feel the Madonna's presence everywhere, in the plants, the cliff faces, the crisp mountain air. She was there in his tent, helping him lift off the galaxy of universal grief. Maybe she even took on physical form, to visit Jason personally, in the guise of the Swedish family, dog and all. In that moment, he had never felt so loved.

As daylight continued to slip away, Jason started to worry. "They should have been back by now. They still have to hike a mile to the 30-foot cliff. They won't make it back by dark." Then doubt started to take over. "Maybe she wasn't the Madonna. Maybe they were just regular people. I hope something didn't happen." Mild panic started to creep into Jason's thoughts, so he bid Dale and Sylvie and brief adieu and ran up the trail to find them.

When he rounded the corner to the head of the canyon, he saw it was wide open. It was only a few hundred yards across. Everything was visible. It wasn't possible to hide a family of three with a dog. But he couldn't see them. Frantically, he ran from one side of the canyon to the other. They weren't there. No dog, no kid, no husband, no Madonna. There were no footprints, no sounds, no signs. They simply disappeared in the twilight. Jason was slowly overcome with the surreal feeling he had just been visited by angelic beings.

He gave up his search in disbelief and headed back down the trail. As he rounded the corner, he clearly saw the silhouettes of Dale and Sylvie in the distance. When he arrived back at camp, he asked them if they had seen the Swedish family. Bewildered, they gave him a baffled look like they didn't know what he was talking about. Jason figured they were stoned to the point of brain mush and let it go at that.

After a very peaceful night's sleep, Jason marched back up the canyon to continue his search at first light. Nothing. The Swedes positively were not there. When Dale and Sylvie rolled out of the sack, Jason asked them what they thought happened to the Swedish family. Dale and Sylvie simultaneously replied, "What Swedish family?"

Jason let the subject drop and didn't mention it again. However, he had a bounce in his step and a whistle on his lips the entire hike back to the trailhead. He was deeply grateful for a magical healing, a lighter heart, and a personal encounter with his very own angels.

Jessica

Besides working at the hospital, Jason was also in the process of building his private practice as a healer. It was the time when social networking was making its initial explosion on the Internet. Jason was reading a marketing book. It recommended contacting anyone he could remotely remember and sending them a friend request. Once you had friends, you could send them a bunch of information they didn't want.

Jessica was one of the hundreds of people he contacted. Jessica and Jason were sweeties in high school…sort of. It wasn't steady but they had a few unforgettable interludes. Jason was a senior, a hormonally driven high school jock. She was a cute and innocent little freshmen cheerleader. Jason tried not to think about their less than morally upstanding encounters when he hit the "send friend request" button. He guarded his embarrassment with the thought, "Well, I was young. With any luck, she won't remember it the same way I do. After all, men are pigs, and boys are worse. I was only being what I was."

Jason vividly remembered the first time they met. It was early fall quarter and he was standing in the hall, grabbing a book out of his locker. All of sudden, he heard from behind, "Hiiiiiii." He turned his head. It was Jessica, looking at him all starry eyed. He slowly turned away and thought in mild disgust, "Oh Gawd, a freshman." Then, in the blink of an eye, his subconscious mind took over and started processing information. "Wait a minute… Freshman…Blonde…Hot…Bold." Before he knew what hit him, some extraterrestrial force snapped his head around for one of the biggest double takes known to the human species. (He still needs chiropractic adjustments on his neck from time to time.) He then beamed an enormous smile and was smitten. He thought, "Wow. Being a senior is gonna be great."

Fast forward 20 plus years.

When Jason sent his friend request to Jessica, he really hoped she wouldn't think he was some creep from the past, stalking her on the Internet. Because that really wasn't the case. It just sort of turned out that way.

Much to Jason's surprise, she responded in writing. She simply wrote, "Hi, nice to hear from you." Jason instantly knew she was available. All of a sudden, he was standing in front of his high school locker again, this time on the World Wide Web. He wondered if Jessica was the new love from the psychic lady's prediction.

Since Jason had last seen Jessica, she'd really filled out her resume. Here were just a few of her sterling attributes: Child Prodigy Ballet Dancer, Actress, Choreographer, Director, Symphonic Musician, Vocalist, Lead Collegiate Cheerleader, Model, Aerobics Instructor, Honor Student, Loving and Devoted Mother, Sexpot, Ambitious, Big Hearted. She was trained on the East Coast and rubbed elbows with some of the biggest names in show business, from New York to San Francisco. To sum it up, she was the full package.

However, her life wasn't one big bouquet of roses. Her precious performing career abruptly ended when she blew her knee out on stage, at the age of 40. She hadn't danced in well over a year. There were a few days when she hit some pretty deep emotional lows.

As Jessica and Jason e-mailed back and forth, they learned they were both bouncing off woeful points in their lives from failed relationships. Each were in their own version of the shambles. Jason was emotionally beat up from his divorce and living in a dungeon of an apartment. Jessica was emotionally distraught from her separation, the end of her career, and the physical injury from her fall. However, they also discovered a shared interest in spirituality and healing. What transpired over the next two years turned out to be remarkable. They were able to help each other heal. It gave their reunion a quality of feeling deeply fated.

After about four weeks of back and forth e-mails, Jason and Jessica decided it was about time for a visit. Her parents lived in Seattle and she was planning a visit from Chicago, in the not-too-distant future. "Plus," she said, "a little drive north will offer a much needed break from my parents." She also added, "While I'm there, do you think I could have a session? I'd love to see what you do." Jason balked but eventually agreed, admitting the idea made him a bit nervous.

Guide - Madonna Two
Even though Jason dumped a load of universal despair in Paradise Valley, he was still in the throes of divorce. Waves of grief still rolled in from time to time and quite naturally, he gravitated to Nature for solace. His favorite place to go when he was hurting was the village of Glacier, Washington. It's located at the base of a majestic volcano by the name of Mt. Baker, or Kulshan by the native people. Surrounding forests contain sacred old-growth mammoths of fir, cedar and hemlock. The nearby river, the North Fork of the Nooksack, cascades off of Mt. Baker's snowfields and serves as a highway for native salmon runs. The pristine glacial run-off is some of the cleanest water on the planet.

There was a small unmarked trail that led from Glacier to the North Fork. It was only known to locals and a handful of whitewater kayakers who used it for a take-out. Winding about a quarter mile to the river, the trail was a cathedral of enormous trees that seemed like they wanted to open up and speak in deep ancient voices. Jason felt the magical ambiance of healing, as if it were hanging in the air.

He came to this trail frequently to unleash his sorrow, because the river and forest so graciously took it off his heart. The greatest healing secret he discovered was in the frigid waters of the Nooksack. Whenever he placed his bare feet in the icy river, pain and sadness drained from his soles and flowed down the river. It was absolute magic and it worked every time.

The trip to Glacier on this particular day was necessary, indeed. It was the day of Jessica's first visit and Jason was exceptionally nervous. It seemed way too soon. After all, he'd only been separated a few of months and wasn't even officially divorced. Entertaining any type of woman was crazy he thought, even one he already knew. What was worse, he woke up that morning with an overwhelming wave of divorce grief. It all felt like exceptionally bad timing. He certainly didn't want to dump any of his crap on Jessica. So as soon as he hopped out of the shower, he headed for the healing waters of the Nooksack.

Jason was deeply soothed when he returned to the trail. He'd strolled this stretch from Glacier numerous times and had never seen anyone on the path. Not even once. That was part of the draw: healing in solitude. Within a few hundred feet of the trailhead, he felt the trees begin to lift the burden inside his heart. Immediately, he was overcome with an enormous feeling of gratitude. It was so strong, it nearly brought him to tears. As he continued down the path in a meditative state of thanks, he heard someone coming in the opposite direction.

It was a woman, approaching from around a slight bend in the trail. She seemed to materialize out of the mist that was lightly suspended in the forest. And she wasn't alone. She was quietly singing to a little boy she was carrying on her hip. He looked to be about three or four years old. Jason stepped aside and exchanged a friendly greeting as they passed.

Jason directly went back to his meditative walk of gratitude and the woman returned to her singing. As they sauntered along in opposite directions, Jason thought he heard her sing, "Remember, we are always there for you." He snapped back around, only to catch a glimpse of them as they vanished around a bend in the trail. He thought to himself, "Nah...couldn't be," and kept on strolling toward the river.

When Jason arrived at the cobbled beach of the Nooksack, there was a volcanic rock about the size of an ostrich egg, split straight down the middle. It was at the immediate end of the trail, where the path emptied out onto a gravel bar. You couldn't miss it. Jason was also a geologist. He'd banged on and cracked open many a rock. The giant egg-rock in front of him was very unusual. He couldn't remember breaking one open so neatly.

He knelt down and opened the split rock like a book. Much to his surprise, on each half of the stone were mirror images of a silhouette that looked exactly like Madonna with Child. In the same instant, Jason was overcome with the fragrance of roses. Puzzled, he stood and stared up the trail. Then, he stared at the river and the gravel bar. He'd been in this place a hundred times and it wasn't until that precise moment, the light bulb switched on. This was on the cobble beach from his vision with Anandaji.

Stunned, he realized he had just been visited by Mother Mary and Jesus, the second Madonna from his vision of long ago. Quickly, he snatched the rock and sprinted up the trail toward Glacier. He ran up and down the two-street village, stopping into every business, asking if they'd seen a woman with a kid on her hip. Everyone in town just shook their head. After an exhaustive search, he came to the conclusion they'd vanished, just like the morning mist hanging over the valley. With his head spinning, Jason realized he just had his second angelic visit in less than a month. With a level of excitement that can only be created by a genuine miracle, Jason jumped into his truck, drove home, and awaited the arrival of Jessica.

Triangle Five

As soon as he walked into his apartment, Jason received a text from Jessica letting him know she was en route and only a few hours away. Nervous anticipation suddenly overwhelmed his excitement from the recent miracle. It was an odd mix of emotional states to come home to. He also remembered the Madonna rock in his daypack, pulled it out, and placed it by his bed. He had to squeeze it in next to the misfit pyramid pieces and noticed how the spiritual hardware was starting to pile up.

He had a few hours to kill before Jessica arrived and didn't know what to do with himself. He nervously paced around for a while, took a shower, paced around some more, and finally checked his e-mail. There was a message from Ula. She said she'd be passing from Seattle to Vancouver and wondered if she could stop by and see the triangles. Jason's first reaction was, "Geez, when it rains it pours. Months of loneliness and isolation interrupted by a deluge of visitors, all at the same time. I smell a little Divine synchronicity in the air."

When Jessica arrived, Jason immediately morphed into a shy eight-year-old little boy. He blushed varying hues of red as he welcomed her in. He actually pinched himself to make sure the moment was real.

He was astounded to see she looked nearly identical to the pictures in his memories: blonde, hot, bold. The only difference he noticed was that she walked with a slight limp. However, as he gazed a little closer, past the facade of her sparkling blue eyes, he could see she had experienced her own world of suffering as well. "Hmmm…," he mused to himself, "It must be tough being a beautiful woman."

Jessica was smart too. She knew the perfect way to break the ice. Cutting through the awkwardness of a long anticipated reunion, she said, "I brought you a gift. I picked it up at a New Age bookstore. I thought it might be right up your alley."

Feeling guilty from not having a gift for her, Jason self-consciously accepted the gift. He held it in his hands and just stared at it.

"Well?" she pushed, "Aren't you going to open it?"

"Oh…yeah…okay," Jason mumbled as he gently tore into the wrapping paper. Slowly pulling the underlying tissue paper away, he froze, as if he were pierced in the heart by an arrow.

"What?" Jessica squeaked, as her voice nervously cracked. "Don't you like it?" Unexpectedly, she felt the bottom drop out of her world, like crumbling and shifting sand. She feared her enormously anticipated reunion was about to collapse.

"No…no…no. That's not it. It's wonderful. Thank you," he said, trying to comfort her. But it was obvious the gift struck a very deep nerve. Jason was obviously dazed. Trying to shake himself back to normal, he continued to unwrap the gift. Gingerly, he took a deep breath and slowly pulled out another golden triangle.

The triangle Jessica gave to Jason was to similar to the one he received in the mail, after his trip to Fiji, almost fourteen years ago. It had 21 mysterious moving symbols on the back, like all the others. It was also slightly thinner and lighter. On the sides, tabs extended like puzzle pieces. Jason was sure it would fit the three-quarter pyramid, unlike the triangle with the blinking eye Anandaji gave him. On the front, was an image similar to the interlocking Venus and Mars symbol on the third triangle. Jason now understood that image represented his former relationship with Pia and the emotional growth it produced. However, the triangle Jessica gave Jason, only had one symbol on the front. It was the same Venus and Mars, formed from one circle, not two. The arrow of Mars was the two o'clock position and the cross of Venus was at six o'clock. Instead of representing a link between a man and a woman, Jason guessed it stood for a true spiritual union.

Jason took a big gulp of air and looked at Jessica with an expression of acceptance. He knew she was going to play an integral role, not only in his life, but also in the unfolding saga of the triangles. So he spent the next few hours filling her in on the details of his triangle adventures, the upcoming visit from Ula, and the recent miracle on the Nooksack.

When the conversation came to a pause, Jason said to Jessica without hesitation, "Let's see if your triangle will complete the pyramid." Without any reverence or sacred fanfare, Jason picked up the three-quarter pyramid, handed the triangle to Jessica, and said, "Here, you do it."

Jessica's eyes widened, as she pulled back and said, "My triangle? Are you sure? This is your thing."

"Not anymore," Jason replied, as he thrust the triangle into her hand. "There. Just put it in like a puzzle."

Jessica gasped as the triangle powerfully sucked into place. Gradually, but forcefully, it filled the room with a warm and soft pinkish-gold hue. It radiated an energy that triggered the kundalini in both of them. As soon as the triangle was firmly attached, Jason placed the newly formed pyramid on the floor, in the far corner. Next, he turned out the lights and let the illumination fill the room. What happened next with the pyramid remains a bit of a mystery because Jason and Jessica had their attention focused elsewhere. They spent the next 36 hours in an aura of passionate lovemaking, that would have left the followers of Kama Sutra green with envy.

Ula's visit
Jason pried his eyes open and slowly rolled over to take a peek at the alarm clock. "Holy shit!" he exclaimed, waking up Jessica as his eyes popped open. He threw off the covers and said, "C'mon, we gotta get movin'. Ula's gonna be here in an hour!" Jason dashed to the shower while Jessica ran a brush through her hair and dusted on some makeup. Within in minutes, they scrambled out the door and made it to the airport with less than a few minutes to spare.

Staring out the windows of the airport, Jessica and Jason were impressed to see Ula's plane gracefully float in like a pelican, effortlessly touching down on the runway. At that moment, Jason realized he'd never seen a private jet land at their municipal airport.

In fact, the arrival of Ula's jet was so novel, it created a minor stir of excitement by a few locals in the waiting area.

Jason was surprised to see Ula get off the plane by herself. He assumed Hakeem would be with her but he was in Geneva on Council business. She was dressed in blue jeans and a simple fleece top, the embodiment of down-to-earthiness, in spite of her colossal affluence. In Jason's limited encounters with her, he'd never seen her put on an air of pretentiousness. She was too honest and secure for all that non-sense.

Ula greeted Jason with a warm embrace and promptly turned her attention to Jessica. The two of them hit it off like peas and carrots and didn't stop yakking until they got into town. Apparently, Jessica and Ula had mutual acquaintances from Broadway.

Jason barely crammed everyone into the cab of his short-bed pickup and drove to his favorite hole-in-the-wall cafe, Mt. Bakery. Once they were seated, it didn't take long for Jason to inquire about Ula's visit. "So...what shakers and rollers are you meeting in this part of the world?" he snooped.

She looked at him with blatant astonishment and said, "You're such a joker. You just can't see yourself, can you? And yes, I did meet with Melinda Gates in Seattle and I'll be meeting with a spiritual society in Vancouver tomorrow. But the real reason I'm in this part of the world is to see you." That comment put Jason back on his heels.

"Jason," she went on, "the Unity Council has known for quite some time, we're preparing for a transformative spiritual event of enormous magnitude. We're not sure when it will be but we think it's still a ways off, maybe as much as a few years. However, everything seems to be accelerating, so there's no guessing. However, we do know there is a timing component involved. When the planets and people are lined up, it will happen.

"Over the past year, it's been revealed to us that there will be a man and woman involved. It's believed they reside in America. When I saw you at Oneness University a few months ago, I suspected it might be you. However, when we spoke, it seemed pretty clear your marriage was on its last legs. So, I thought, it couldn't be you. Then, when I heard about your triangles, my suspicion was revitalized. And now that I see you here with Jessica, I have no doubt."

Jason's heart skipped a beat. "What? Jessica and I are supposed to be part of a far-reaching spiritual movement? I don't think so. I can't handle that. It's too much responsibility." Jessica gently placed her hand on his forearm in reassurance, as if she'd known all along. Jason suddenly felt coerced by the entire universe. It was going to take some major soul-searching to wrap his head around this one.

While the three of them continued to converse, Jason noticed a group of college students sitting in the far corner of the cafe. They were busy spying on Ula. Staring obsessively, they couldn't stop whispering in amazement. One of them pulled out her phone, snapped a photo, and began texting like a maniac. That's when Ula caught them out of the corner of her eye and shook her head in mild annoyance.

Jason turned back to their conversation and filled Ula in on the events since India: divorce, miracles, triangles, and Jessica. When he finished, he looked at her with reverence and said, "We haven't tried to attach Anandaji's triangle to the pyramid yet. Remember, the one I showed you in Pondicherry? Would you like to give it a go?"

Without blinking an eye and holding the presence of nobility, she replied, "I'd be honored." So without further ado, they stood up and headed out of the cafe.

As soon as they stepped outside, they were greeted by reporters from the local newspaper and television station. They wanted an interview with Ula. Apparently, the college kids in the corner had recognized her. They were also newspaper staffers at the university and thought it would be a great idea to contact the local media.

Jason gently grabbed Jessica's arm and wheeled her away. He looked back over his shoulder and barked, "Ula, we'll meet you at the truck." As they scurried off, Jason turned his head and heard the reporters grilling Ula about the Unity Council. Totally perplexed, Jason asked out loud, "How the hell do they know about the Unity Council?"

*

When Ula finally caught up with Jason and Jessica, they crammed back into his truck and headed to Ula's hotel. When they arrived, Jason toted her bags up to the room. Taking advantage of the spectacular afternoon, the three of them wandered out to the balcony, to enjoy the view of the bay. As soon as they sat down, Ula felt obliged to explain the situation back at the cafe.

"Last month the Unity Council met in the rolling hills of Tuscany in west-central Italy. In some of our meetings over the years, we've been visited by ascended masters and saints who have offered tremendous guidance and direction in our mission. Yet, they've always manifested energetically, that is, without bodies. On more than a few occasions, they've been channeled by our seers. However, the last meeting was the first time we were visited by a master in physical form. It was St. Francis of Assisi; brown robe, tonsured haircut, stigmata, the whole nine yards.

"He appeared during the first group meditation. It took everyone by complete surprise. As an introduction, he spoke briefly about the importance of general spiritual values, such as compassion, forgiveness and simplicity. Then he performed a number of miracles and healings for individual members of the Council. When he finished, he promptly walked outside and strolled down to the local village, as if nothing could be more natural. When he arrived at the village square, he started performing miracles without saying much at all. It didn't take long for the entire square to be overrun with on-lookers. When he had the entire crowd's undivided attention, he stating talking about the Unity Council and the important role it was playing in global transformation.

"To top off the entertainment, at the end of his discourse, St. Francis disappeared into a ball of brilliant white light. If that wasn't enough, the fountain in the center of the square (which had been dry for years) began to flow like a geyser. That little stunt sent the crowd into a frenzy. From that moment on, it was referred as an honest-to-God, hallelujah, apparition, à la Catholic. Needless to say, the Italian media jumped all over it.

"Furthermore, numerous people videoed and photographed the event with their cell phones and posted them on the Internet. Oddly enough, all the imagery of St. Francis came out grainy and broken up. The only thing preserved, with any quality at all, was his voice. That technical glitch put extra emphasis on his message about the Council and it went global, instantly. In other words, The Unity Council's cover has been blown."

Jason stood up and leaned on the balcony rail, trying as hard as he could to disregard the implications. He didn't say a word. He simply gazed at the bay for a few frozen minutes. With great resolve, he drew a deep breath and turned his head toward Ula. With a smirk on his face he said, "So, you ready for that triangle?"

The Oracle
It was unanimous. The best place to attempt the next triangle fitting was in Ula's suite. Jason left the two ladies to froth over their newly found friendship, while he headed back to his apartment to pick up the goods.

As he pulled his truck onto the arterial, Jason started to feel the weight of his possible global destiny. It had all been fun and adventures up to this point. But now it seemed to have taken on an enormity beyond his wildest imagining. He was a nature boy of solitude, not a man for the masses.

The route back to his apartment passed under Interstate 5. Jason thought to himself as he approached, "If I get on I-5 and head south, I can be in Mexico in a couple of days; if I go north...Alaska?...The Arctic Ocean?" Either alternative sounded better than the pressure of a global spiritual revolution. He remembered from high school history, revolutions usually ended up with somebody's head in a basket.

When Jason returned to Ula's suite, he unceremoniously pulled the pyramid and the triangle out of his daypack and began to unwrap the contents. He'd fished an empty yogurt container out of his recycle bin to use as a stand for the inverted pyramid. If all went well, they'd eventually be turning the pyramid into a diamond-shaped octahedron. They just had to keep finding triangles.

The pyramid was still pulsing a pinkish-gold energy. It blasted a surge of kundalini power into the room when Jason flipped it over and placed it in the yogurt container. He gave Jessica an amorous, seductive glance and pumped his eyebrows a few times to tease her. She gently slapped him on his bicep and quipped, "Naughty boy."

Next, our heroes sat themselves around the dining table in Ula's sizable suite and closed the drapes to the balcony. Ula pulled out scarf and placed it in the center of the table. Jason placed the yogurt container holding the upside-down pyramid on the scarf. Next, he pulled out Anandaji's wrapped triangle.

As he peeled the paper towel away, everyone became exceedingly tense. What they were attempting seemed far too significant for such an unacquainted group of mortals. They simply didn't know each other well enough. Suddenly, Ula shouted, "Wait! Let's do this at sunset. It will give us time to get ready." As soon as those words were uttered, everyone breathed a collective sigh of relief.

They spent the rest of the afternoon, decompressing and strolling along the bay. Jason eventually went ahead on his own little adventure, while the girls did some shopping in a few bayside shops.

Jason found a secluded corner on beach between some boulders and tried to steady himself. "C'mon, c'mon, stay in the moment, stay in the moment." But he couldn't do it. All he could see were the culminating facts. He had magical triangles. He was personally involved with people of enormous wealth and influence, who were on a global mission. They thought he was a key player. When Jason tossed it around in his head, part of him was genuinely honored and excited. Another part of him wanted to vomit from all the perceived future stress. "C'mon, man, stay in the moment."

Then he had an idea. "I'll give the pyramid to Ula." Instantly, his mood buoyed up and he trotted back along the bay to meet the ladies. When he told the girls of his brilliant idea, Ula didn't hesitate.

"No way, Jason. This is your gift to the world. Only you and Jessica can walk this path. There are some crucial steps you still need to take before you can give it away. The magnitude of this universal gift can only come through someone who is highly evolved. Fail or succeed, this is your fate. However, Hakeem and I, as well as the entire Unity Council, will help you in any way we can."

Jason's heart sank into the pit of his stomach. He felt like he had just been scolded for trying to chicken out on his destiny. He was numb. He didn't feel like an evolved soul, just scared and heavily burdened. If that wasn't enough, he wondered how his new relationship with Jessica would hold up under the strain.

After a few minutes of awkward silence, Jason gave a deep sigh of resignation and said, "The sun's starting to go down, let's head back."

*

When they cracked the door open to Ula's suite, the sun was falling behind the distant islands. The softening sky dimmed into a rich palette of pastel hues. Jessica pulled out a scented candle she had purchased from one of the shops. She lit it and set it next to the inverted pyramid. Ula fired up her laptop and turned on her favorite meditation music. Glancing around at each other in the moment of finality, the three of them took a deep breath. Ula said, "Here we go."

Jason led a brief meditation to help ease the tension. When they were deeply relaxed, he unwrapped the triangle and handed it to Ula. The eye in the pyramid was blinking noticeably. Jason stabilized the yogurt container with his hand and Ula carefully moved the triangle toward the upside-down pyramid.

It fit perfectly. As it wavered and melded into the place, the pinkish-gold hue and pulsing kundalini energy collapsed. It formed a golden ball of light, about the size of a golf ball, hovering in the exact center of the future octahedron. For a few moments, everything stopped. It felt like the impending doom in the eye of a hurricane. Then, a beam of luminescence slowly rose from the golden ball and entered the blinking eye of the newly attached triangle. From there, it acted exactly like light passing through lens of a movie projector.

From the center of the eye, light shot out into the room creating four separately distinct three-dimensional movies. They all hovered in air, like a futuristic cinema. None of them were in color but were in monotones, sepia, black and white, bluish-green, and golden. Instead of flat screens, the movies were in spheres. There was no sound but plenty of action.

The sepia movie-orb unveiled the history of the planet, from creation to present. The images came from vastly differing civilizations, ecosystems, landforms and climates. There even appeared to be a civilization, far advanced from their own, that vanished long ago without a trace. However, it wasn't all unfamiliar. They recognized a few cultures and locations. But most were far removed from their understanding of history.

The black and white movie seemed to be a potential future. It was ugly, dark and frightening, filled with lack, disease and violence. The scenes were so disturbing, they made Jason nauseated. He tried to focus his attention on the other movies, so the Armageddon-like monstrosity wouldn't register in his subconscious.

Like the black and white movie-orb, the blue-green globe appeared to be a potential future. However, it was filled with life, creativity, health and well being. It was a world where people lived in harmony, not only with each other, but also with the planet. It was a world Jason wanted very much to be a part of. As he glued his eyes on the unfolding of events in that future, his heart was illuminated with a soft glow of joy.

The golden movie was clearly from another reality. Jason couldn't find any words in his vocabulary to do it justice. There were images he'd never seen before, triggering emotions he'd never felt before. It was beyond breathtaking. Furthermore, he guessed he was only seeing a small percentage of what was presented. There was an entire level of experience he couldn't grasp. It was simply beyond his capacity as a human being.

As Jason deepened his hypnotic fix on the movies, they slowly spun and moved around the room. They commonly overlapped and intertwined with one another. The areas of overlap created entirely new scenes. Each movie had a direct impact on the other.

Jason took a few steps. He noticed the movie of the past had changed. He took a few more and saw the movies of the futures change. Same with the angelic movie. Each time he changed his angle of view, the movies changed accordingly. He could alter his view of reality simply by changing the way he looked at it. When that realization ignited his gray matter, he understood the movies were conveying a basic underlying truth. "Maybe," he thought, "that's how the entire Universe works: perception creates reality."

The light show concluded when all of the movie-orbs coalesced back into a single sphere. The golden ball of light supplying the power slowly diminished and the movie orbs disappeared. At the same time, the blinking eye dissolved into the golden structure of the newly attached triangle. Nothing was left but the upside-down pyramid, its newly attached triangle, pointing at an angle toward the ceiling, and a plastic yogurt container. However, Jason could still feel a powerful vibrating energy, radiating off its golden framework.

When Jason, Jessica and Ula came back to earth, the girls were quite shaken. Ula urgently wanted to make sense out of everything and discover the underlying meaning. She was certain there was a message in it for the Unity Council. Jason, although moved, took it in stride. He'd be through a number of these surreal events before. His take on the experience was completely different.

"Ula," he said, "we've just experienced something far beyond human comprehension. It's not our job to figure it out. That's much too big for us. After all, trying to figure the world out has made a mess of things. In my opinion, what just happened was an end in itself. Our golden geometric object is a sacred tool of teaching. Only it's not the kind of teaching we're used to. It's emitting coded messages, simply through the act of existing. It's here to help us. Our job is to experience it as it is. That's it. In that act, our world will be positively transformed."

Jason could see she was having a difficult time digesting the concept. After all, she was a shaker and a mover. The idea of experiencing, assimilating and waiting wasn't in her DNA.

Jason continued. "Ula, it's not that difficult. As humans, we have a natural tendency to complicate things. All we have to do is relax, experience it, and soak it in. The rest will take care of itself. Action will flow when the timing is right. If you don't believe me, go ask the Council. See what they think."

When he finished his mini-sermon with Ula, Jason took another look at the upside-down pyramid with the attached triangle pointing upward. Thinking out loud, he said, "It sure looks kinda funny. It's no longer a pyramid and it's not yet a diamond. What should we call it?"

Jessica piped in and said, "Let's just call it what it is."

"And that would be...?" Jason asked.

"An Oracle."

"Sounds good to me," Ula approved.

"Me too," said Jason. "Oracle it is."

With that decided, Ula invited Jessica and Jason to stay the night in her suite. That was an easy invitation to accept. Lively conversation continued well into the night, until drowsiness and gravity took over. Then, the three of them drifted off to sleep, amidst the energy of the radiating Oracle. It was one of their most memorable night's rests ever.

*

Ula's flight departed at 11:00 the next morning. They only had time for a quick coffee on the way to the airport. Over coffee, Ula invited Jason and Jessica to the next Unity Council's meeting in Iceland. "I'd like you to come as featured guests," she said with welling pride.

Jason looked at Jessica in panic. He didn't know what to say. Uncomfortably speaking for both of them, he said, "Thank you... but..ahh...we'll have to wait and see. A lot can happen between now and then. But please keep us posted." Ula giggled at his lack of commitment. She could see he was nowhere near ready for the big stage.

It was a heartfelt and tearful goodbye at the airport. It seemed several lifetimes had been lived in the past 24 hours, creating an unbreakable bond between them all. As Jason and Jessica watched Ula's plane lift off the tarmac, Jason leaned toward Jessica with affectionate eyes and responded to the ambience of the moment. He gave her a big sloppy kiss.

Jessica Blooms
After Ula left, Jason and Jessica returned to their lives and their long distance relationship. Jessica was off to Chicago while Jason went back to his healing practice and the fallout from divorce.

Jessica kept a routine of visiting Jason once a month. Each time she visited, she dove into private healing sessions with him. Jason observed she had the natural ability to go into a very deep state of meditation. She also and had a tendency to drift out of her body. He was so impressed by her incredible spiritual talent he suspected her healing would progress notably and rapidly. It did.

Over a few months period, Jessica permanently released some deep-seated subconscious fear. Jason had never seen so much initial success, with accompanying side benefits, from just a few sessions. She said much of her success stemmed from one decision. She wanted her spark of vibrancy back; she wanted to live.

Essentially, Jessica was born again. She was working out in Pilates, strengthening her knee, and actually dancing again. A doctor told her a year before, even if she had a full knee replacement, she'd be lucky to walk normally. She proved them all wrong. Dance, her truest first love, turned out to be the best medicine of all.

Jessica had a natural connection to God she experience frequently as a child. It happened whenever she danced. To her, dance was a moving meditation. As she continued to heal, she was able to restore that connection and incorporate it into other facets of her life. Over the course of that winter, she discovered a very keen and sharp intuition. Her channels of communication opened so widely to the other side, she became flat out psychic. She discovered numerous guardian angels and guides, which she accessed regularly for counsel and information. Furthermore, the more she learned to trust her gift, the more her gift sharpened.

She also developed the art of manifesting, better than anyone Jason had ever met. She could visualize something she desired, ask the Divine for help, and...boom...she'd have it within a week. A house, an office, money and people to connect with. It was uncanny. It was like she could just snap her fingers and things would appear. Jason eventually had to admit, he was a bit envious.

News of Pia
Between visits from Jessica, Jason maintained a very full life. Outdoor recreation was near the top of his to-do list. He went hiking whenever he could. On one beautiful summer Sunday, Jason took a hike near Mt. Baker with Michael, a buddy he'd known for quite a while. They were members of a local hiking club when Jason was married to Pia. However, Jason left the club soon after they split up. He noticed other members of the group felt obligated to pick sides. Jason wanted no part of that; it was far too painful.

After about three miles of a moderate ascent through old-growth forest, Jason and Michael pulled over for a water break. As they small-talked away in the shade of a giant hemlock, Michael suddenly blurted out, "Pia's moving to Sweden."

"What?" Jason replied, as stoically as possible.

"Apparently, she fell for some Swede at a meditation school. Sorry to drop the bomb man, but I thought you should know."

Jason was shell-shocked. All of a sudden, everything made sense and he thought, "It was that guy she was with at the temple. She met him in Sweden when I was working in Canada. All of her trips to Oneness were to see him. How could I be so naive? She's been screwing him all along."

Jason felt completely duped. Then he felt sick and said to Michael, "Thanks for the info bro, but I gotta go home and lie down." And that's what he did. When he got home, he plopped on the sofa and didn't move for the next 15 hours. At one point, he pulled out the Oracle for a bit of solace. It was a nice try but it didn't work. He was back on the roller coaster of grief.

Vision - The Goddess
In an attempt to keep his grief at bay, Jason forced himself to practice some meditation. The physical exhaustion created by his emotional anguish allowed him to drift into a very deep trance.

As Jason sank deeper and deeper into a state of relaxation, he thought he caught a faint stench of raw sulfur, burning the inside of his nose. At the same time, the temperature in the room was rapidly escalating. Jason became extremely uncomfortable; his heart rate soared while beads of sweated dotted his brow and ran down his back. As the temperature and stench continued to swell, orange sparks began to fly through the air, as if being shot from the floor. Soon sparks were shooting everywhere. Putrid smoke billowed from below while the sound of a gigantic combustible furnace roared to a deafening pitch.

Jason was terrified, confronted with the overwhelming primeval force of the planet. It was the same force that inspired ancient civilizations into "The Fear of God." He also to knew this was it and panicked at the thought of an untimely death he was not ready to meet. He shot a glance at the floor below, as it began to burn the soles of his feet. The ground glowed in shades of yellow, orange, red and black. It began to move as it broke apart, like unstable melting pack ice. Steadying to draw his final searing breath, he realized he was in the magma chamber of a volcano.

Without hesitation, the volcano erupted with the force of a nuclear explosion. Instantly, Jason was propelled in a river of burning magma, down a gently sloping mountain. As the river of fire gushed downhill, Jason bobbed along like a cork in bathtub. Horrified, gasping for breath, and astounded he wasn't being consumed in flame, Jason futilely screamed for help, over and over again, until he was limp with exhaustion. Within moments, he was flushed into the brine of a salty sea with an enormous *HISSSS*, accompanied by underwater implosions and a gigantic plume of steam.

Jason must have blacked out because the next thing he remembered was opening his eyes and staring at the expanse of a star-filled sky. Floating on his back and entranced by the beauty of the night sky, he saw the last of the eruption sputtering in the distance. As the sizzling in the sea began to die down, he thought he heard voices several hundred yards down the beach.

He rolled over on his belly and swam toward the sound. He raised his head and saw a campfire in the far blackness of the beach. When he reached the end of the solidified lava flow, he turned and swam for land. The shore next to the cooled lava was a beautiful black beach that twinkled in the starry night. He gingerly pulled himself to his feet and began a slow saunter toward the flickering campfire.

The voices in the distance were definitely engaged in an intense rhythmic chant. Cautiously, he continued to move closer under the cover of darkness and stopped about 50 yards away to assess the situation. They seemed like ancient Polynesians, dancing around a ritual fire. Each dancer wore a carved wooden mask with a different, yet very intense, human emotion. Suddenly, Jason didn't feel safe. He began a nerve-racking silent retreat, not knowing where he could hide in the blackness of the beach. Fear seized his body, unaware if the warrior dancers were friend or foe.

As Jason fears escalated, the entire band of dancers stopped and stared in his direction, informed of his presence by their collective sixth sense. Immediately, they picked up torches, shields and spears and sprinted directly toward him. As they rapidly approached, Jason saw molten red magma in their eyes, beneath their wooden masks. Horrified, he turned and ran but was immediately overtaken in the sand.

The terrified Jason was hurried back to the bonfire. In the center of the fire was a large stone of solid basalt. Protruding straight up from its center was a wooden stake, designed to burn sacrifices to the Goddess of the volcano. They had been waiting for him. They knew he was going to show up in the darkness.

There was a path through the fire, making a clear passage to the stone alter. Kicking and screaming, Jason was dragged and tied to the stake, facing the volcano in the distance. Feverishly chanting, the dancers hurled fuel onto the fire and danced themselves into a frenzy. As they stoked the fire, Jason watched the volcano on the distant horizon. The sputtering magma in the cavities of the mountain gave the exact impression of a beautiful, omnipotent Goddess.

As the flames of the fire roared, the dancers chanted at the top of their lungs to the volcano deity. Jason howled from the primordial center of his being, as flames leapt up and scorched his skin. The sacrificial offering raged into an inferno and Jason was consumed by the overwhelming sacred conflagration.

The next thing Jason remembered was lying in a heap on his bed. All he managed to do, when he finally came around, was roll over onto his back. He knew the Goddess was his next spiritual guide and wondered how long it would take her to show up in this physical world.

Chapter 9
Power

When Jessica learned Jason bottomed out with another wave of grief, she had an idea. "I think we could both use a vacation," she said, trying to cheer him up. "How about a little trip to Hawaii?"

"What's that again?" he said, not believing the sound coming out of his phone.

"Just for a few days, of course. I know a great little bungalow on the north end on Kauai. It's right on the beach."

"I don't know, Jess" Jason resisted, refusing to be pulled out of his funk. "I'm not really the tourist type. I'd do much better in the Australian outback or on an Alaskan fishing trip."

Jessica retorted in defense of Hawaii. "Jason, you don't understand the nature of Hawaii. In terms of spirituality, it's one of the most powerful places on the planet. Earth energy is constantly being poured onto the surface through volcanic lava. There are very few places like it; Iceland, Greenland, Yellowstone and maybe a handful of others. Hawaii is a spiritual powerhouse."

"Really?" Jason replied, surprised the idea had never dawned on him before. He thought it over for a moment. Another spiritual adventure sounded quite appealing. Plus, it might get him insight to his recent vision. "All righty then," he said. "You win. When do you want to go?"

Welcome to Hawaii
The evening before his departure, Jason started packing. Staring at his laptop, he couldn't decide if he wanted to take it or not. Suddenly, an e-mail announcement popped up. It was from Anandaji. Jason couldn't believe it. He'd never received one from

him before. He quickly clicked it open and read, "Be on the lookout for new teachers. They may not be wearing bodies."

"That's weird," Jason thought. "I wonder if it was even is from Anandaji. It sounded more like a fortune cookie. However, I must admit, the timing is a bit suspicious." Trying not to read too much into it, Jason responded in his usual mode of lengthy cyber discourse and typed, "OK." Then he turned off his laptop and decided, "That's it. This implement of distraction is staying home."

The five-hour flight from Seattle went without a hitch. Jason and Jessica had a short layover in Honolulu before connecting to Lihue. When their row number was called to board the plane, Jason dutifully got up and plodded into line, like a cow headed for slaughter.

As he slowly inched forward, he saw a blurry vision of a wooden Hawaiian mask. He strained his awareness to focus in on it. The mask was narrow and tall, about three feet from chin to brow. It was carved from dark exotic hardwood into the face of a warrior, complete with a furious expression and razor-sharp teeth. Behind the mask was molten lava, vitalizing the eyes and mouth into a living blaze of red. It was hard to tell but it seemed to be about 10 feet away, suspended head-high. Without warning, the mask charged at the speed of lightning, slammed into his torso and exploded. Jason gasped and stepped back, as he eyes burst open in horror. "What the hell was that?" he screamed.

Everyone in line turned around and stared at Jason like he was nuts. Jessica looked on apprehensively. She knew something was up. Jason quickly faked a cough, trying to conceal his impending state of shock. He glanced around at all the rubbernecks and waved his hand in dismissal saying, "Sorry everybody…got something caught in my throat." Then he looked over to Jessica and silently said with glaring eyes, "What are we getting ourselves into?"

She shrugged in embarrassment, as if to say, "Oooops."

Welcome to Hawaii.

Reamed
On the flight to Lihue, Jessica took one look at Jason and immediately raised the back of her hand to his forehead. "Are you alright?" she said. "You look a bit pasty."

Jason could feel a fever coming on. Droplets of perspiration were beading along his hairline. "I'll be okay. I just need a nap. Whatever that was back at Honolulu sure gave me a bit of a start."

By the time they reached their bungalow, Jason's shirt was soaked in sweat. He was also extremely agitated and couldn't sit still. "Damn it," he said, as he paced around the room. "I feel like I've been possessed by the Tasmanian Devil. All I want to do is go hunt wild pigs."

Jessica was overrun with dread. Her idea of a spiritual vacation was resting in tropical bliss while sunbathing on the beach. She could see with Jason, it meant dancing with his demons. Before she unpacked her clothes, she was already thinking about catching the next plane back home.

Jason continued his pacing until he could stand it no longer and bolted out the door for the beach. He spent the rest of the evening pacing around on the pristine sand, like a caged tiger. Every unresolved emotion remaining from his divorce was purged through the pores of his skin.

Jason didn't return to the bungalow until well after dark. Jessica was sick with worry. When he stumbled in through the screen door, he was wiry-eyed and ragged. He looked like he'd just been released from a prisoner of war camp. Jessica cautiously approached. Once she decided it was safe, she gave him an intense hug.

"You okay?" she asked.

"I'll make it," Jason responded. "Boy, whatever nailed me back in Honolulu sure meant business. I just got the emotional reaming of a lifetime."

Guide - Hawaiian Goddess

The next morning, Jessica treated Jason to brunch at one of the swankiest resorts on the north shore. Sitting on the upper terrace, they had a beautiful view of the rolling surf and the rainforest mountains in the distance. Jason felt, more or less, back to normal. Jessica was greatly relieved his storm had passed and started to slip into the carefree bliss she had come for.

At breakfast, Jason was able to ease into the moment. A beautiful sunny day, an unparalleled setting, delicious food, and a beautiful companion. It really was paradise. As he surveyed the distant scene a little more closely, he froze in mid-bite of his waffle and dropped his fork to the floor. The mountain forming the horizon was the Polynesian Goddess from his meditation a few weeks before. He immediately remembered he had been burned at the stake in that little episode and almost soiled himself on the spot. Reaching over and squeezing Jessica's hand to reassure himself, he knew this was going to be no ordinary mainlander's vacation.

When Jason and Jessica arrived back at the bungalow, Jessica had the rest of her holiday planned out in detail. Couch, deck, beach, deck, couch. Repeat. Jason, on the opposite side of the spectrum, was still wired from his airport incident and knew he was under the influence of some Hawaiian deity. In the recesses of his mind, he defiantly challenged the Goddess to bring it on. That turned out to be a bad idea.

As Jessica hunkered in for phase one of her vacation, Jason went for a stroll along the shore. It was a beautiful day. A stiff breeze filled the air and the surf was very high. There was a rainbow in the distance, arching from the forest out onto the sea. A few seabirds circled overhead, complimenting his view of Eden.

Jason set his gaze down the beach, as far as he could see. He guessed it was well over two miles until the shore wrapped around a modest headland. As he continued to look around, it dawned on him. "Where am I?" he thought. "Hawaii...right? Tourist destination of millions. Where then, for God's sake on this picture perfect day, are all the people?" There was nobody, not even a loose dog or a wild chicken. Jason didn't know if it was a miraculous blessing or a sign of imminent doom. In either case, he felt the hair stand up on the back of his neck.

As he rounded the corner into the adjacent bay, Jason saw someone sitting on the upland side of the beach, near the edge of the beach grass. It was a woman, a Hawaiian woman. She was seated erect in deep meditation. She was attractive, yet her stature exuded uncommon strength. With one glance in her direction, Jason thought to himself, "Woo, there's some power." He saw she was both fully feminine and masculine, at the same time. He immediately altered his course, giving her a wide berth. He didn't want to disturb her, or even look at her for that matter. Her presence was too intimidating.

When Jason was just about past, he spied her out of the corner of his eye. Her eyes and mouth instantly flashed a fiery red, as she blasted a hiss like a vampire. The warrior mask that attacked Jason at the airport burst back to life inside of his chest. He unconsciously let out a shriek and sprinted for the sea. When he reached the water's edge, he turned back around to the meditating woman. She wasn't there.

"Okay! That's it!" Jason roared to the Goddess. "Enough! I quit! You win! Now, leave me alone!"

He stood shaking and barely moved for the next hour. He just paced back and forth on a small stretch of beach. It wasn't until some children arrived with plastic shovels and buckets that he felt it was safe to leave.

As Jason walked back to the bungalow, he felt a fire burning from within. He wasn't sure what it was and prayed it wasn't harmful. At first, the sensation stressed out his already taxed system. But with each step toward the bungalow, he felt stronger and more confident. When he arrived, he was surprised to find, he was wearing a beaming smile.

Depression

The next couple of days Jason went hiking, kayaking, biking, snorkeling and anything else that kept him moving. He felt revitalized and very alive after his walk on the beach. Conversely, Jessica remained within a 100-yard radius of the bungalow, moving from one reclined position to another.

On day three, Jason finally coaxed Jessica to join him on a short kayak-hiking excursion to a sacred waterfall in the central part of the island. According to Hawaiian legend, it was where souls entered and exited Kauai.

When they arrived at the put-in, Jason was disappointed to see it pandered exclusively to tourists. That certainly put a dent in the holiness of it. Fortunately, no one else was there and Jason hoped they'd get to visit the sacred site in private.

The voyage to the trailhead was only about a mile of flat water. The overhanging vegetation provided a tropical mystique, as they slowly paddled their course upstream. When they reached the final corner and made the turn, Jason's spirits plummeted to see thirteen other kayaks pulled up on the muddy beach. "Great," he thought, as their kayak ran ashore, "there goes the neighborhood."

It was a balmy slog up a muddy trail. The trail ran alongside a creek. As they progressed up the path, Jason thought it was a bit odd they hadn't seen anyone. After all, there were plenty of kayaks at the trailhead. When the trail finally veered from the creek, it made one last minor ascent to the waterfall. As he suspected, Jason heard voices in the distance.

When they peered over the rise, Jason was disgusted. People were screaming and whooping it up in the pool beneath the waterfall. Beer cans were strewn all over the place and it seemed half of the crowd was stoned and/or drunk. Clothing appeared to be optional.

"Fucking idiots," Jason muttered under his breath to Jessica. He was saddened and furious at the same time. "How can those frickin' morons be so disrespectful? This waterfall has been sacred turf for centuries. They're ripping it up it like a trailer-trash hot spring. Clueless."

Jason immediately turned around with Jessica and walked the quarter mile back to the creek. They bushwhacked another 100 yards upstream and plopped down on the bank. Jason was pissed off beyond belief. For a while he just sat and stewed. Jessica sat behind him on a rock and massaged his shoulder for a few moments. Jason rolled his eyes up to Jessica and said, "I think I need to meditate for a few minutes. Do you want to join me?"

"No thanks," she said. "You go ahead. I'll just wade in the stream for a little."

Jason found a perfect tree, sat down, leaned back, and closed his eyes. He relaxed to the sounds of overhead birds and the bubbling creek. Within moments, a presence cloaked his energy field. It felt like a wet blanket, lowered over his entire aura. It was so vivid he sprung up and tried to shake it off. Jessica, seeing he was finished with his meditation, crossed back over the ankle-deep stream.

"Uh-oh," she said, as she stared at his face. "What just happened?"

"Nothing," Jason said, as he shook his head.

"Something happened," she said. "I can see it in your eyes."

"I'm okay," he retorted, in mild annoyance. "I'll be fine by the time we get back to the boat."

He was wrong. With each step he took, he sank deeper and deeper into a heavy melancholy. Jason had known depression before but this was a different beast altogether. This depression wasn't his. This sadness belonged to somebody else. It felt like the hopelessness from an entire subjugated culture. He wondered if this was how native Hawaiians felt about the desecration of their holy sites.

By the time Jason made it to the kayak, he was done in. It took every ounce of strength to paddle back. In all honesty, Jessica did most of the work. When they reached the bungalow, Jason crashed on the couch and curled up in a fetal position. He didn't move until morning, not even to eat. As he lay there under the weight of eternity, all he could think was, "I can't believe this is happening in paradise."

Triangle Six
The next morning, Jessica tried to entice Jason off the couch with the idea of fresh pastries down at the coffee shop. No luck there. She was becoming increasingly worried and was running out of ideas. So she did what any sane person would do. She went to breakfast by herself.

When she returned, she chimed out as cheerily as possible, "The barista at the coffee shop said sea turtles hang out in the little cove around the corner. It's just down the trail, a little ways past the parking lot."

Jason sat up with a gargantuan effort, trying to summons a positive response. As soon as he was upright, he burst into tears. "What is wrong with me?" he sobbed into Jessica's bosom. She had no clue. All she could do was attempt to console him. After a few moments of gentle caresses from Jessica, Jason lay back down and went fetal. He was dead weight until late afternoon.

Jessica was down at the beach when Jason finally pried himself off the couch. He grabbed his snorkeling kit and forced himself down to the small cove. There was nothing there, just water and large rocks forming the shore.

He jumped in with mask, fins and snorkel and floated around in the chest-deep pool. He didn't know what he was looking for because he'd never seen a sea turtle before. He expected to see a little critter about the size of a skillet, like the ones at Harden's Pond he used to catch as a kid.

If he didn't see any turtles, that was fine with him. Floating weightlessness in the lagoon help ease the depression. "Maybe I'll stay here all night," he thought, lying on his back, watching the clouds.

Jason was mindlessly watching sea grass dance on the seafloor, when a sea turtle effortlessly cruised in on collision course, banked a slight right-hand turn, and drifted by like the Starship Enterprise. Jason flailed for the surface and gasped for air, beating a hasty retreat to the nearest rock. "Whoa, that was huge! I wonder if they bite." Then another turtle drifted in. Then another. Jason watched as they hoisted themselves out of the water, onto smooth boulders on the other side of the cove. It was obvious how docile they were.

Jason jumped back in. Soon, a few more drifted in from the open sea. Jason was mesmerized, watching them glide by within an arm's length. Within 30 minutes, he counted fourteen new arrivals. However, he was starting to get chilled and thought, "One more, then back to the bungalow."

He placed himself in the center of the entrance, well positioned for incoming traffic. As the next turtle sailed in, Jason could see it was the biggest one yet. However, as it banked a turn and drifted by, he saw something hanging out of its mouth. "Poor thing," Jason pitied. "Looks like he got snagged by a fishing lure." Turning to watch it vanish into the turbid water, he saw the lure fall from its mouth. Jason slowly drifted over, hovered above, and saw it partially covered on the cove floor.

"Aha, buried treasure," he gloated like a greedy pirate. Then he dove and grabbed the booty off the silty bottom. It was getting dark and his mask was fogged up, so he couldn't make out the details. However, one thing was for sure. It was a lot bigger than he originally thought. He swam to shore and hoisted himself onto a rock, like a turtle. When he lifted his mask, he couldn't believe what he held. It was another golden triangle.

Jason hurried his loot back to the bungalow to show Jessica. He didn't say a word. He just held it up, like a fisherman showing off his latest catch. In telepathic unison, they stared at each other in disbelief. Simultaneously, they shook their heads and said, "Not now…no way."

With that said, Jason tucked the triangle into the secret pocket of his suitcase, then rolled up into a ball of depression on the couch.

Depression Goes Poof
The next morning was departure day. Jessica packed her things with a sigh of bittersweet resignation. She didn't want to go back. Jason couldn't wait to get the hell out of paradise. He was still carrying the depression like a dead weight.

When they arrived at the airport, they were greeted with a five-hour delay. The battery on the airplane died. Jason figured it was a perfect symbol of his "vacation." When they finally settled into their seats on the plane, Jason was still weighted down with enormous sorrow. It was so heavy, he seriously wondered if the plane would get off the ground. However, within five minutes of lift off, the depression vanished. It felt like an angle lifted it off his shoulders. It was remarkable. From that moment on, it was bon voyage depression and good riddance Hawaiian deity. However, Jason hadn't seen the last of the Goddess yet. In fact, they were just getting acquainted.

Mr. Tick

Jason and Jessica parted at the Seattle airport. Jessica flew back to Chicago and Jason caught a short shuttle north. They agreed the next triangle fitting would have to wait. Jason also knew the triangle was a reflection of his personal growth. The pot got a major stirring in Hawaii. He needed time for it to settle out.

Not long after his return from Hawaii, Jason took a solo hiking trip to the arid side of the Cascade Mountains. It was early spring. White covered the tops of the surrounding peaks but the lower south-facing slopes, sprouting with wildflowers, were free of snow. Much to Jason's delight, there wasn't another soul in sight. He had a four-mile stretch of trail to himself. His only companions were sagebrush and over a hundred wintering mule deer.

About half way into his hike, the sun broke through the clouds. It was the perfect opportunity to soak up some early season rays. So he pulled up a patch of earth, tossed off his jacket, rolled up his pant legs, and sprawled out on the ground.

Within a few minutes, he entered the twilight zone, halfway between sleep and awake. Appearing out of the mist of his consciousness was the Hawaiian Goddess. She hovered emotionless in his mind's eye. Her appearance intensely radiated unadulterated power. Jason's body trembled. She extended her right hand and placed two fingers on the top of his skull. All he felt was her light touch. Then, as quickly as she appeared, she vanished.

Jason's eyes popped open and he sat up. He wasn't sure the apparition was real. It could have just been random thoughts, left over from Hawaii. He didn't want to think about it, so he shifted his attention to a nearby herd of deer. Then he stood up and finished his hike.

About five days later, Jason was cruising down the dairy isle of the local food co-op when he scratched his head. He stopped walking in mid-scratch and felt a bump where the Goddess had placed her fingers. Aggressively, he dug his fingernails into his scalp and pulled out a wood tick. "Damn," he said to himself, "that little bugger was really in there. Must have picked it up on my hike. Better keep an eye on that spot." Then, he carefully dismantled the tick and flipped the remains in the garbage.

Two weeks later, Jessica was coming for another visit. When Jason woke that morning, he noticed not one, but two, bumps swelled up on his scalp. They were exactly where the Goddess had placed her fingers. One was about the size of a pea. The other ballooned into the size of a jelly bean. Later that afternoon, when Jason met Jessica at the airport, he bent over a said, "Look, I've grown bumps."

"Oooo, that doesn't look good," she said, examining them more closely. "Is that where the tick bit you?"

Jason nodded with bravado.

"We should probably drain it," Jessica continued. "It looks infected." As soon as they got to Jason's pad, that's exactly what they did. It was disgusting.

The next morning, Jason went in for his monthly massage. Afterward, when he was walking back home, he noticed an ache in his Achilles heel. By the time he arrived to his apartment, he was dizzy and feverish. That night, he broke out in a raging fever, followed by bone-rattling chills. Fever and chill battled back and forth throughout the night. By the following morning, he was delirious and badly dehydrated. Jessica had seen infectious diseases before and immediately scurried him off to emergency. This was grave business, indeed. She also canceled her commitments in Chicago and planned to stay for the long haul.

Over the next three days, Jason slipped in and out of delirium, accompanied by extreme fever and chill. Teetering on the edge of a coma, he knew he was on death's doorstep. He was oblivious to his external surroundings. However, what he saw with his inner mind was exceptionally lucid. It was a threshold of brilliant white light, open to the other side. The pull was magnetically intense. He desperately wanted to go but instinctively knew it wasn't his time.

Nonetheless, he willed himself out of his body. It wasn't until he looked down at himself that he realized how sick he was. "Wow," he thought, "I'm almost dead." As he continued to rise up, he saw a silver umbilical cord attached between the navels of his physical and spiritual bodies. He didn't know what it was but guessed it some kind of safety rope.

Jason completely left his body and floated toward the threshold. With eyes closed, he passed through the door, engulfed in brilliant white light. When he arrived on the other side, he slowly opened his eyes to what he assumed would be heaven. Much to his surprise, it wasn't St. Peter. No sir, it was the Hawaiian Goddess; unflinching, powerful and magnanimous. School was in for Jason.

Lesson 1 - Shape Shifting and Totems
The first thing Jason noted was the Goddess neither spoke nor moved. Intuitively, he knew exactly what she was teaching. She was also suspended in space, with a universe of stars as her backdrop. Eternity was Jason's new classroom. He figured since he was there, he'd better pay attention. He hoped when (or if) he returned, he'd have new tools to use in the land of the living.

Jason had difficulty adjusting to being out of his body. It didn't feel right. For starters, his hands and feet were itching like crazy. That seemed odd, because he wasn't physical. As he examined his hands more closely, he noticed they were quickly growing coarse black hair. In fact, hair was growing everywhere; face, arms and back. It consumed his chest and crawled up the back of his neck. If that wasn't weird enough, his body ballooned, trembling and quaking, until it ripped through his aura. His feet transformed into massive paws. At the same time, he was possessed by a primeval ferocity. He knew what was happening. Through a magic almost extinct in the modern era, Jason was transforming from human to Beast. He was shape shifting.

Immediately, he dashed through the cosmos, leaping from star to star, like a madman. As he raced through space, he quickly shifted his inner focus, from Beast to Eagle. In mid-stride he sprouted wings and feathers and soared through the stars of the galaxy. Next, he was Shark. Then Otter. Lion, Penguin, Snake, Whale, Monkey. Simply by focusing his attention on an animal, he instantaneously adopted their attributes and form.

He knew, from that moment on, he could access animal totems in meditation. Their importance became perfectly clear. If he could become an animal in meditation, he could bring their traits back into the three dimensional world. He could become Bear to fight off injustice and protect his family. Otter for playfulness and fun. Fox to outwit an opponent. The applications for totem energies were endless. He further learned, animal totems send signs by showing up in your physical world, approving the use of their power. Jason was using animal totems at Chevron Mountain. He just didn't know he was doing it.

Lesson 2 - Bilocation
When Jason had his fill of shape shifting, he drifted back to the feet of the Goddess for more instruction. Next, she powerfully focused her unwavering gaze. Jason watched a pulsating orb of color form on the center of her forehead. With continued focus, her energy intensified. Suddenly, Jason saw not one Goddess but two. Then four, then eight, then sixteen. Before she multiplied again, Jason understood what to do and nodded his head.

Jason closed his eyes and focused his attention between his brows. By using intention and concentration, he moved a small sphere of vibrant energy into his third eye. When the sphere was ready, he projected a beam of light. Forming in the near distance, like a dancer in the spotlight, was an exact replica of himself.

He was amazed how easy it was to be in two places at the same time. Then, he transferred his awareness back and forth between himself and the newly formed Jason. Within a few moments, both Jasons had their own independent identities. A few moments later, he was standing face to face, having a conversation with himself.

Both Jasons quickly recognized how this trick could come in quite handy. With that lesson learned, they looked to the for Goddess approval. She blinked her eyes and nodded her head, as they slowly fused back into one self.

Lesson 3 - Manipulation
As soon as Jason settled back into a single entity, the Goddess's aura began to billow, like an enormous thunderhead. She was summoning power from the source of Creation itself. Jason was terrified. He was sure it was the second coming of the Big Bang.

The cosmos lit up behind her, like a gigantic movie screen. First, he saw the parting of the Red Sea. Next, an enormous mountain chain tumbled into the sea, followed by a forest, sprouting to life through a parched dessert floor. Last to come were the masses of people. Everyone had strings attached like puppets. They moved this way and that, as armies, political parties, and social reform movements. Each was bending and swaying to the will of the Goddess.

"No!, No!" Jason screamed in horror. She was teaching him how to manipulate the forces of Nature and People. The scariest part was she was showing him how to override the free will of others. All he had to do was focus his intention.

"I won't do it," he violently protested. "I'm not ready. It's too much responsibility. I am not God!"

The Goddess roared Jason back into submission. "This is your path. Mastering the world of spirit comes with this power. You cannot avoid it. However, if you ever choose to override the will of Nature or People, it must never be done for self-gratification or ego. It must be in alignment with Divine will. If you falter, the karmic backlash will be severe. Furthermore, you can never truly know Divine will. You can only know It in the aftermath of your actions. Selfless service leads to soul evolution. Selfish egotism terminates in suffering, for you and others."

Jason defiantly refused to practice. He didn't want the gift of an overpowering will. He was too afraid of the consequences. However, as much as he didn't want it, he could feel the power welling up in his abdomen. He instinctively knew he could move it with ease.

*

The instant Jason mastered his new talents, the Goddess vanished. In the same breath, the silver umbilical cord in his navel illuminated and blasted him through time and space at warp speed. He shot through the threshold and slammed back into his physical body.

He gasped a quick puff of air and quickly opened his glassy eyes. Nurse Jessica was there, softly gazing down, loving, nurturing and concerned. Stroking her palm on the side of his face, she said, "There you are. Welcome back. I thought we were going to lose you there for a minute." Then she gave him a peck on the cheek and gently placed a fresh cold pack on his forehead.

At first, Jason didn't respond. He couldn't. He was too weak and sick. It took every ounce of strength to eventually say, "Thank you. I'll be okay. I think the worst is over." Then he rolled over and fell back into a sleep for the dead. For the next month, he barely got out of bed.

It took Jason seven months and a treasure trove of antibiotics to beat the infectious tick bite. However, the threshold to the Goddess's teachings remained wide opened. Jason's gifts were there, waiting to be used.

Triangle Six Revisited
Jessica's trips to visit Jason extended with each passing month. It wasn't long until they were practically living together. So they

decided to rent a love loft, while Jessica transitioned from Chicago to the Northwest.

It had been several months since Jason went comatose to visit the Goddess. He'd regained the majority of his strength and was nearly back to normal, except for the continual relapses that came when he went off antibiotics.

Because his health was unstable, Jason wasn't able to go back to work. That gave him time for his spiritual pursuits, like the sixth triangle. He and Jessica had been studying it for weeks and noticed it was much different than the previous five. The only similarity was the 21 mysterious symbols moving on the back. On the front, there were no symbols, text or glyphs. There was just an image of a face that changed frequently and at random. Each new face gave off its own unique vibe.

Most of the faces Jason and Jessica didn't recognize. They seemed like old souls form ancient and forgotten times. However, a few images stood out. There was one Jason thought was a dead-ringer for Jesus. Jessica recognized another as Saint Theresa from one of her Sunday school books. Another looked like the Native American shaman, Sun Bear.

The physical nature of the triangle was also very different. It was translucent, comprised of an otherworldly, lightweight material somewhere between golden light, oil and plastic. Jason played with it for hours, passing his hand through it only to watch it regain its shape. It reminded him of lava lamps, he saw as a kid. It was incredibly hypnotic and soothing.

As he sat on the couch playing with it, Jessica stated the obvious. "You know, when we attach the triangle to the Oracle, it will want to go public. That's its nature. It's bigger than the two of us."

Jason nodded. "Yeah, I know. But let me try it my way first and see what happens, if you don't mind."

"Whatever works for you. I'm with you all the way," she replied.

With that agreement under their belt, they decided it was time to attach the latest triangle.

To relax the mood, they went through the usual routine. They made a tiny alter, put on soft music, dimmed the lights, and lit some incense. Without pomp or circumstance, Jason lifted the Oracle, as Jessica moved the triangle into place. Instead of fitting it like a puzzle piece, she simple let it go. It drifted perfectly into position, like a feather settling to the ground on a windless day. There were no fireworks, no light shows, no bells, no whistles. Instead, the entire room was filled with an overwhelming Presence of unconditional love. The strange part was, love wasn't being radiating off the Oracle. Instead, it was being pulled in from all directions. As Jessica and Jason sat facing the Oracle, they were inundated with love energy, entering their hearts, coming in through their backs. It was incredible. The Oracle had evolved into a magnet of unconditional love.

Show Time
Jason had a hard-shell case and a stand made for the Oracle, so he could put it on display in public. His first stop was the city park down by the bay. It was a beautiful summer day and the park was filled with its usual activities. Kids were on the swings, Frisbees were sailing through the air, dogs were walking their owners, and beverages were being sipped at the coffee stand.

Jason set up shop on the north end of the park, away from the all the hustle and bustle. He didn't want the Oracle to get nailed by a Frisbee on its first day out. Working methodically, like a photographer setting up a tripod, Jason set the Oracle on its stand. Jessica put out a couple of foldout camping chairs. Then, the two of them sat back with a cup of tea and waited to see what would happen.

Immediately, the first couple walking by did a major double take and froze. Within 15 minutes, about 50 people were gathered around. The Oracle's presence was powerfully mystifying. It sucked people in like moths to a porch light. If it weren't for the sea breeze and the kids at the other end of the park, you could have heard a pin drop. However, a few on-lookers were absolutely repelled and felt obligated to voice a few obscenities as they passed.

The Oracle also put off some type of invisible protective barrier, about 10 feet in diameter. Instinctively, everyone respected its sacred space, especially children and dogs. Jason was very surprised no one approached to look at it more closely.

As time passed by, Jessica and Jason felt unconditional love being pulled in. From the looks of things, it seemed others were experiencing it too. Each man, woman and child that stopped to look on, helped the Oracle's power grow.

For most who stopped, the experience was deeply transforming. Some openly expressed affection to the person they were with; others beamed with joy, some shed a few tears, and everyone felt more connected to each other. Collectively, it was an extremely moving experience, far more, Jessica thought, than a Broadway performance of *Les Misérables*.

After about an hour, the energy created by the Oracle faded and the crowd dispersed to their sunny afternoon. As Jason packed up, he grinned at Jessica and said, "My, that went well. We'll have to that again…soon." Jessica agreed and gave him a big smack on the lips.

*

When they got back to the love loft, Jason sent an e-mail to Ula, letting her know the show was now officially on the road. She responded by begging him to attend the next Unity Council meeting. Jason asked if there was any chance of holding the meeting in the States. He knew a great little lodge on Montana's Gallatin River, just outside of Yellowstone National Park.

Within two weeks, Ula had the next Unity Council meeting set for late October, at the Sunshine Lodge on the Gallatin River. It would be the first council meeting in the US. Jason and Jessica were on the slate as featured guests, with the idea of presenting the Oracle.

The two lovebirds knew they only had a few months to show the Oracle before the meeting. So every Saturday they planned a different public venue to let the Oracle work its magic: Seattle, Vancouver, Victoria, Whistler, Portland. The idea got both of them very excited. It was a life-affirming mission they could do together. Plus, they'd get to visit places and meet people they never dreamed of. However, as they busily planned their crusade, Jason had no idea he was poised for a startling brush with his dark side.

Calvin
Seattle…ahhh…The Space Needle, Pike Street Market, the Waterfront, truly the emerald gem of the Pacific…when it isn't raining. Jason had the Oracle set up at a futuristic park on Elliot Bay, just north of downtown. It was nice. There was sunshine, a comfortable sea breeze, and lots of people milling around. Jessica was in Chicago, winding down her affairs, so it was just Jason and the Oracle.

The showing that day was similar to the others. However, the Oracle, assisted by the forming congregation, created a particularly strong presence of love. It seemed some folks were having powerful experiences, maybe a few deep healings. As Jason sat incognito, he decided to join the fun. Reaching into the Hawaiian Goddess's treasure chest, he pulled out one of his unopened tools. He surveyed the crowd and picked a few likely candidates. He wanted to see if he could influence their actions by focusing his will.

He was astonished. By concentrating his thoughts, he got a man to scratch his head, a child to climb into her mother's arms, an elderly woman to gasp at the Oracle. He couldn't believe how easy it was. At first, using his new power of mind control was frightening. But after a while, it was fun. It was like playing with living dolls.

There was one guy in particular who was especially suggestible. He seemed to possess almost no will of his own. Jason could influence him with ease, simply by projecting his thoughts. He was so enamored with his new puppet, he decided he wanted to meet the fellow. So Jason put that thought into the air. Within a few minutes, Mr. Puppet came over and introduced himself. His name was Calvin.

Much to Jason's surprise, Calvin was a multi-bazzillionaire who had made it big with one of Seattle's most successful corporations. It was the computer company behind the PC revolution of the 1990s. Calvin was one of eight ground-floor employees. They brought the whole thing to life, from a dusty little garage in Wallingford.

Calvin was raised outside of Boston by "an asshole of an alcoholic father." Over a couple of decades, his Dad built a sizable storage-unit business. Most of it was backed by money from the mob. When Calvin turned 18, he joined the military to get as far away from his old man as possible. However, living in the military wasn't much different than living with his Dad. So, as soon as he was discharged, Calvin made tracks for the west coast. He fell in with a bunch of nerd-brained, ambitious computer jocks and worked his butt off for ten years. The rest is history.

When Jason met Calvin, he thought he'd hit the jackpot. Imagine having your very own bazzillionaire puppet. The next day, Jason was sitting in a corporate box suite at a Mariner's game. A few days later, Calvin arranged a TV interview for Jason to present the Oracle. Within a week, he'd personally dined with some of the richest people in the world. In no time flat, Jason energetically manipulated Calvin, to gain entrance into the lives of the rich and famous. He loved every second of it.

Calvin and Jason also spent some quality time together, hiking, cycling, kayaking. They almost became good friends, except for one thing. The foundation of their friendship was built on manipulation. That was something the Goddess warned Jason to be extremely careful with.

Several weeks into their "friendship," Calvin had a couple of healing sessions with Jason. They went well for Calvin. However, Jason opened his sacred inner world to him. That was a mistake. Calvin now had the subconscious keys to his soul. Plus, their new relationship was based on deceit. The result of that combination nearly killed Jason. The karmic wheel of spiritual responsibility was turning, and it was about ready to set itself right.

One weekend, Jason and Calvin planned a hike into the Mt. Baker area. When Calvin arrived, Jason was surprised to see a new red pickup squeal into his driveway. From his living room window, it looked like Calvin was extremely irritated. Jason dashed outside to see what the problem was. As soon as he got there, he caught a whiff of Calvin's breath. He'd been drinking. Furthermore, Jason didn't recognize his body language or his speech patterns. This was a completely different guy. Jason had no clue who this Calvin was, not by a long shot.

The conversation in the driveway quickly turned hostile. Jason couldn't say anything to appease Calvin. He was a drunken raving maniac. The only thing Jason could pull out of the conversation was that Calvin's father had just died and he inherited a substantial sum of dirty money.

Jason didn't understand the energy dynamics of inherited money. When someone receives an inheritance, they can become heir to the spirit of the person who died, as well as the vibration of their money. Jason didn't know Calvin had taken on the ghost of his abusive father and his mafia-derived fortune. In a way, he was possessed. Calvin's natural suggestibility turned him into a channel for evil. What was worse, Jason had opened his sacred inner space to Calvin. He was now in the cross hairs of a Calvin's Dad's demonic spirit. A few minutes after he arrived, Calvin sped out of Jason's life forever. All he left behind was the residual of his father's fury.

Jason went back into the loft and literally started shaking. The negative interaction with Calvin was so intense and unexpected, it left him totally frazzled. A few hours later, he felt a strange pain in his stomach. It wasn't an illness, it was something else. It felt like a giant hook had skewered his abdomen, curled around, and pierced the lower part of his sternum. He was a hooked fish, pierced through his third chakra. Unfortunately, he wasn't able to grasp the connection between the pain in his gut and his earlier confrontation with Calvin. That was still a few days away.

At first, his stomach wasn't very sore. It was just annoying and peculiar. However, over the next three days, the pain intensified until Jason couldn't get out of bed. His skin turned a pale shade of blue-gray and he felt the life force draining out his feet. He knew he was dying. Lucky for Jason, Jessica was due to arrive that day.

When Jessica entered the loft, she was horrified. "My God," she thought. "It's another relapse from the tick bite." However, when Jason explained the circumstances, she immediately pulled out the Oracle. Then, she picked up her phone and called New York to contact the most powerful healer she knew.

Working over the speakerphone, the healer proceeded to take Jason and Jessica into a deep meditative state. Within minutes, the Oracle illuminated and Jason felt a tingling sensation in his stomach. Suddenly, the pain subsided and the oppressive evil force was released. The healing was instant and it was nothing short of a miracle.

By evening, the color returned to Jason's skin and his intestines were back to functioning normally. No more poltergeist. Even so, the entire incident gave him plenty of time to reflect. He had abused his spiritual powers with Calvin and learned the karmic laws of cause and effect. Abuse has its consequences. Spiritual evolution is not a privileged status. It's an awakened state of humility. He felt so stupid and sorry, like a kid who refused to heed a parent's explicit warning. He should have listened to the Goddess. Now, he was just thankful to be alive.

Ruth
Jason's next stop with the Oracle was his favorite city, Vancouver, B.C., on beloved Granville Island. Although his approach to displaying the Oracle was the same, his attitude had been altered considerably. He was now a humbler Jason, a wiser and less cocky Jason. Furthermore, he was dead-set against any game playing. He was there to support the spirit of the Oracle, namely, in healing, transformation and awakening.

While Jason was setting up, a few supporters who recognized him from his TV interview in Seattle came up and asked to take his picture. Jason submitted, then graciously brushed them off and slipped into invisibility. For some odd reason, fame and fortune had lost its appeal.

It only took about 30 minutes for a group of about 500 people to gather. From the looks of things, it appeared the Oracle was going to be exceptionally strong. Right off the bat, several people had spontaneous physical healings, and a ring of rainbow light formed the protective perimeter. The entire show morphed into an honest-to-God spiritual phenomenon. About 45 minutes into the event, a camera crew arrived from the local TV station. To avoid detection, Jason simply pulled up his collar and melted into the crowd. As soon as the news team finished its business, the energy of the Oracle dissolved and everyone went back to their lives. If there was any doubt in Jason's mind up to that point, the message now was crystal clear. The Oracle wanted public exposure. Jason, on the other hand, did not.

Jason packed up the Oracle as quickly as he could. However, before he could make a speedy getaway, he was approached by an elderly woman who introduced herself as Ruth. She was rather attractive, well made-up and adorned with expensive clothing and jewelry. Jason guessed her age to be somewhere around 70. Ruth was in a desperate state, babbling on and on about her sick husband. She begged Jason to bring the Oracle to her house to help heal her husband. Just in case pleading wasn't enough, she threw out some bait to Jason's lower nature, by offering a handsome sum of cash.

Jason didn't know how to respond. He took an immediate liking to Ruth and sincerely wanted to help. But Jessica was due to arrive in a few hours and he was already cutting it close. He still had to drive back to the States and allow time to cross the border.

Apologetically, he said, "I'm sorry Ruth. I'd love nothing more than to help you and your family. But my girlfriend is due to arrive in a few hours and I have to pick her up at the airport in Bellingham. I can't be in two places at the same time."

Suddenly, as if hit by lightening, Jason stopped in mid-conversation and said, "Hold that thought. I'll be right back."

Jason scampered into a nearby alley and quickly focused his attention between his eyebrows. Immediately, an indigo-blue ball of energy formed. Without thinking twice, he projected a beam of light and created a replica of himself. Each Jason had its own consciousness and identity. On top of that, a third non-physical awareness was created that linked them all together, kind of like an air traffic controller. What made it even more bizarre was that all three Jasons were aware of each other at the same time.

Jason #1 went about his affairs and headed back to the States to fetch Jessica. Jason #2 returned to Ruth and began the journey of healing her bedridden husband.

Levi
Ruth and her husband Levi lived in West Vancouver. They owned a beautiful home overlooking the Vancouver skyline, Burrard Inlet

and the Strait of Georgia. Over the course of his professional life, Levi had made a killing in real estate. Now he was dying.

When Jason and Ruth arrived, they were greeted by her daughter and a friend of hers from Toronto. Jason was amazed to learn they already knew him from his Seattle news clip.

The overall atmosphere in the home was one of exhaustion and heartbreak. They'd been watching Levi slip away for the past couple of months. Now, they were desperate because Levi was unresponsive. They despairingly wanted Jason to spin his magic Oracle and bring Levi back to the land of the living.

Jason said he would do what he could but needed to meet Levi first. Accommodating his request, Ruth escorted him into the sunroom overlooking the sea, where a bed had been placed for Levi's comfort. As Jason walked in, much to everyone's surprise, Levi sat up and started talking as if nothing could be more normal. It was a miracle.

Jason didn't know Levi had been in a coma for the last three days, so the little miracle went unnoticed by him. He then proceeded to chitchat back and forth with Levi. As the pleasantries came to a close, Jason asked Ruth and the girls for a minute in private and escorted them to the door.

As soon as the ladies exited, Levi dropped off again, this time into an exceedingly deep coma. From Jason's vantage, it appeared Levi was drifting rapidly toward the threshold of light. Like a trained shaman on a mission, Jason entered a deep state of meditation to access some spiritual guidance. Waiting on the other side was an escort from the spirit world. It was Raven. When Jason saw Raven, he understood he'd been called for a specific mission, because Raven accompanies souls back and forth from the spirit world. Without hesitating, they merged souls and Jason absorbed his essence completely.

Jason blinked his eyes several times and regained normal consciousness. After a momentary internal scan, he knew Raven was with him. Moving delicately, he leaned over and whispered to Levi, "It's okay, Levi. You can let go now. Everyone will be alright." Then, with the controlled consciousness of a Tai Chi master, Jason softly stretched out his hands about six inches above Levi's belly. Slowly, his hands began to glow a brilliant golden-white light. The intensity of the light continued to increase until the whole room lit up like Yankee Stadium.

When the light from Jason's hands hit a crescendo, reddish, boiling light bubbled up from Levi's torso. Levi's burning red light went straight through Jason's golden-white hands. The entire room went awash in red and white light. It was so bright, it started burning Jason's eyes and he had to look away. When he could take it no longer, the light died down and the room went back to normal. Jason, very gingerly, said a prayer over Levi, then slowly walked out of the sunroom.

In the adjacent room, the ladies were eagerly waiting for Jason to emerge. They saw the fireworks shining under the door and knew something intense was brewing. Perhaps this American miracle-maker was the real deal. When Jason finally floated out, he didn't say a word. The ladies bolted in to see the awakened Levi.

What happened next would have run a shiver up your spine. Instead of turning cartwheels and bouncing out of bed, singing praises to the Almighty, Levi was colder than lunch meat on a marble table. Jason hadn't resuscitated Levi. Instead, he helped him cross over to the other side. It was a first-class escort to the pearly gates.

Apparently, Levi and his family had some Jewish blood, dating all the way back to the old country. When Ruth realized she hadn't gotten the kind of miracle she was hoping for, she launched into a rendition of *Wailing and Gnashing of Teeth*, unheard of anywhere this side of the Atlantic. It was downright old-world primordial.

It didn't take long for the ladies to recognize Jason had been called in to perform a very sacred act. They were heartbroken but they were grateful. They knew they couldn't let go of Levi without his help.

Jason hung around until the Rabbi arrived. Shortly after, a van from the funeral home showed up to remove Levi's body. Due to the configuration of the staircase, they couldn't get the gurney into the house. So Jason assisted the funeral home roadies in carrying Levi's body out to the van. Not only did Jason have to help Levi exit spiritually, he also had to help him physically.

When all was said and done, it was well past midnight. Jason quietly bid the grieving family adieu and slipped outside Then, he dissolved back into the body of Jason #1, who was now in bed, sleeping with Jessica. Jason #1 was startled awake when his replica re-entered his body. He was relieved to be one Jason again. As he drifted back to sleep, he sent his blessings to Ruth and her family.

Chapter 10
Synergy and Polarity

In the weeks preceding the Unity Council meeting, Jason noticed he'd evolved beyond the level of a traditional healer. He'd now experienced both his dark and light sides. Furthermore, many of his experiences were commonly beyond the norm, including the release of entities, out-of-body experiences, communicating with angelic beings, accurate premonitions, interacting with the dead, and being in more than one reality at the same time. Plus, he also felt more and more in control over the mechanics of the physical world.

As his spiritual prowess continued to unfold, so did his recognition. It was due to the Oracle, which was starting to feel like a monkey on his back. It was becoming a distraction from what he considered most important: his own spiritual evolution. He wished there was some way he could distance himself from the Oracle.

Then he had an idea. He'd dump it on the Unity Council at the meeting. "My toy, my rules," he thought.

It was a couple of weeks before the meeting and Jason was receiving e-mails from Ula every day. According to Ula, the meeting was going to be very well attended by some of the "most powerful people on the planet."

"My God," Jason thought. "I wonder if the Dali Lama will be there. Or maybe the President. Or maybe even Jesus himself." All the hype raised his anxiety to level orange.

Jason also hoped his spiritual growth had elevated to the point where another triangle would appear. There were still two more to go until the Oracle was complete. The meeting seemed like the ideal place to manifest a new one. Except for the fact, he didn't know how the process worked. It was obviously rigged by an intelligence much greater than his own. After all, he never dreamed he would have to wait 14 years between triangles three and four. He was growing tired of the obligation, now that it was going public. Plus, he disliked being in large crowds. Maybe if the last two triangles appeared, he could get free of it for good.

Then he had another idea—group manifesting. He'd let that one loose on the Council too.

Vision - Chief Three Forks
The Unity Council meeting was to be held in a refurbished barn, on the banks of the Gallatin River. It was beautifully crafted in western log cabin motif and the lodge used it regularly for wedding receptions. There wasn't a better venue for a spiritual gathering anywhere in the valley.

To get there, Jason had a long drive in front of him. He was going to pick Jessica up at the Bozeman airport, crossing three states and four substantial mountain passes. As he made his decent into Bozeman, he passed through the region of Three Forks. Three Forks is where the Missouri River branches into its three main tributaries; the Gallatin, the Madison and the Jefferson. It was critical decision location for the Lewis and Clarke Expedition. It was there they decided to follow the Jefferson River upstream, to get them to the Pacific Ocean.

As Jason cruised along the open highway, he felt a strange tingling sensation moving up his spine. He immediately felt dizzy and pulled off the highway onto a dirt road. He got out of his truck and laid down next to a stream. He was extremely lightheaded and felt like he was about ready to pass out.

He closed his eyes for a moment and smelled the aroma of pine and fir trees nearby. When he reopened his eyes he was startled to find his gaze open to endless panorama of stars, stretching beyond the silhouetted reach of the trees. Day had instantly transformed into night. In the distant blackness, he could hear the muffled roar of a small cascading mountain river.

Jason lowered his eyes and scrutinized the darkness in front of him, to see something...anything. As he strained his perception into the vacuum of light, he thought he saw the flash of a spark. Then another. Soon a small flame began to grow into a sizable and well-kept campfire. He could smell the wafting fragrance of dry cedar, as the fire crackled and danced into life.

Soon the fire was ablaze, kicking off a much welcomed, penetrating warmth. Jason stared at the light of the fire, dancing off surrounding rocks and trees—illuminating the periphery with a flickering yellow glow. He turned his gaze into the fire, drifting deeper and deeper, until he synched with the rhythm of Nature. He was drifting back in time, to a time far removed from the mechanical and electronic inventions of the human mind, when the Spirit of the Earth was tangible and very much alive. Then, he saw what looked like a human, standing outside the light cast by the dancing fire.

Jason was neither alarmed nor frightened. He felt the strong spirit of the slowly advancing human, just as he felt the spirit of the surrounding rocks, river and trees. This creature was a piece of the living planet. He was as much a part of Nature as the mountains, forest and sky.

As the human pulled into the light of the fire, Jason saw it was a man. And this was no ordinary man. He was a Chief, decked out in ceremonial attire of Natives from the American Midwest. He wore a magnificent wardrobe of finely ornamented buckskin, with an eagle-feather war bonnet that reached nearly to the ground. He carried himself in a dignified aura of majesty, an unmitigated splendor of the human species. To Jason, it was clear. He was being visited by a supreme Archangel.

What happened next took Jason completely by surprise. The Chief began to speak, or rather, plea. In an ancient voice that commanded complete respect, he told his story. His face was earnest and unmovable as stone. Furthermore, his impassioned communication indicated his life, as well as those he loved, clearly depended on what he was about to speak. However, as the Chief continued to articulate, Jason couldn't understand a word he was saying. Instead, he had to interpret the message through the tone of his voice, animated hand gestures, and heart-felt facial expressions.

Jason shuddered in humility and wondered, "Why would a being of such stature be speaking to someone like me, especially in such a desperate manner?" The whole scenario made Jason deeply uneasy. He thought he was being called upon to shoulder a responsibility that was far beyond his capacity.

Nevertheless, Jason became sincerely captivated, as an audience of one. The Chief began his soliloquy by introducing himself and his heritage. As he continued, Jason could tell the Chief was describing the plight of his people. With each story the Chief told, Jason noticed, the Chief was growing larger. The more forceful and passionate he became, the larger he grew. The lower half of his body merged with ground below, turning his legs into the roots on an enormous tree. As he continued to expand, the Earth trembled and the fire collapsed. Soon, the Chief was only visible from the waist up. The remainder of his body was underground. From the ground to the top of the Chief's head was at least eight feet. Jason held fast, holding off his panic in the surreal moment. His attention was fixed on the vehement story line of the Chief.

As the Chief fervently continued, Jason saw his stories in the reflection of his eyes. They were an endless silent movie reel, shifting from one horrific event to another. Jason was aghast at the revelation of violence and cruelty, seen through the eyes of the Chief.

It wasn't until that moment, Jason realized the Chief was not a representative from a particular tribe or nation. He was the spiritual voice of them all. His story captured the horror from every subjugated, imprisoned and annihilated culture throughout history. Through the Chief's eyes, Jason witnessed the endless procession of conflict, broken promises, enslavement, intentional spreading of disease, massacres, death marches, resettlements, desecration of entire ways of life, and the breaking of the spirit of a people. The countless sagas of horror rolled in, one after the other. When the ghastly reminiscence finally ended, the Chief paused his narration and openly wept for what seemed like an eternity.

When his tears dried, the Chief lifted his head and looked Jason squarely in the eyes, communicating a truth far surpassing any horror from his ancestral past. Never, for one moment, through murder, separation, or imprisonment, had people ever been separated from the Earth. That connection has always been the road to the soul. It's the gateway to the future. People...belong to the Earth.

From that moment on, the Chief was transformed. He was now a visionary seer. A new story was in his eyes, a story of a future. However, it wasn't a future of technology, in a society removed from the rhythms of the Nature. It was a vision of Spirit returning to the lives of its people. Harmony and balance had been restored. Nature was revitalized to support the lives of its inhabitants, in an endless flow of healthy give and take. And it happened because people rediscovered the lost art form of ancient cultures, the art of listening to the Earth. Through the Chief's eyes, it was a possible future of beauty, the Great Spirit working hand-in-hand with the Earth and its people.

However, the Chief's eyes turned stern, to clearly relay another message. The possibility of this magnificent future is just that...a possibility. Success or failure lies in the hearts of people. A positive transformation is only possible if humanity looks inside itself and heals the inner maladies of the heart. Healing the fragmented human spirit will restore fullness. But it's a warrior's path of great courage because people will be required to take responsibility for their own self-inflicted suffering. Furthermore, the Chief made it abundantly clear, they must also remember the Spirit of the Earth. Plus, there was no time to waste and very much to do. And…this was the only way.

With his last message conveyed, the Chief slowly shrank back to normal size and stood in the fading light of the fire. The expression on his face and the gentle motion of his hand, clearly said to Jason, "I have done all I can, the rest is up to you." Jason stepped back in guarded reluctance and his small shoulders ached with the burden. The transference of the Chief's hope felt like the unbearable weight of a very large and unstable world. Jason knew he was no Atlas.

Without speaking another word, the Chief dissolved and was magnetically pulled into the dying fire. Soon, there was nothing left but the pop and crackling of the flame. As the Chief disappeared, Jason listened closely. He thought he detected the final mumblings of the Chief's fading voice. A voice that sounded very much like a deep supplication of wholehearted prayer.

As the flame died out, an enormous column of thick billowing smoke rose up. When it hit the atmospheric ceiling, it spread laterally, covering the entire sky. The unyielding billow then thrust downward, in a violent convection cell of burnt particulate. Jason gasped and coughed, as the entire forest became clogged with smoke. He felt like he was trapped in a burning building with no escape. His eyes burned, as he waffled to his feet. He staggered through the pitch black forest, stumbling on rocks, bushes and fallen trees. Escaping the smoke was futile, so Jason sprawled on the ground, hacking and coughing while trying to use forest floor duff as a face mask. Within minutes, his oxygen supply was nearly exhausted. There was nothing left to do but surrender himself to his inevitable fate. With a last attempt at a gasp for breath, he reluctantly let go of his grip on life and lost all forms of consciousness.

When Jason came back around he found himself pulling into the parking lot of the Bozeman airport.

Guide - Chief Three Forks

Jason had just enough time to fill Jessica in on his vision when they reached their destination on the Gallatin River. Jessica had a vision of her own on the flight up and they were both convinced the upcoming meeting was of major significance.

However, when they arrived they were surprised to find the lodge very quiet. They were expecting throngs of followers. However, Ula indicated the Unity Council wasn't very well known in the US. For Jason, that was very welcome news.

Jason and Jessica had been to the lodge once before and were familiar with its wildlife theme. Each suite was named after a different animal, such as Otter, Sandhill Crane and Eagle. When they checked in, the attendant at the front desk was proud to announce they would be staying in their newly redecorated room, Chief. When they opened the door, the first thing Jason noticed was a portrait of an Indian Chief hanging over the fireplace. It was the Chief from Three Forks. Jason and Jessica clearly felt his presence, which remained strong throughout the entire weekend.

Conditions

The meeting was to begin precisely at sunset, so Jason and Jessica had a few hours to kill. Furthermore, Ula asked them to hold off on socializing until the meeting started. She said that would help focus and strengthen the energy. So they went on a drive toward Yellowstone and saw bighorn sheep, blazing autumn colors, and the mountainous grandeur of Montana. They returned to their room just as Ula arrived.

"Everyone ready?" she beamed with all the excitement of a stage manager.

"You bet," Jessica, the former cheerleader, echoed back.

Jason just nodded and gave a very nervous grin.

"Great," Ula perked. "I'll be back to get you in about an hour."

Jason spent the next 60 minutes pacing a hole in the carpet.

About an hour later, Ula returned and said, "Everyone is present, ready and in an elevated state of consciousness. Let's go."

Jason immediately started sweating like a pig. On the walk across the lawn to the barn his hands became so wet, he almost dropped the Oracle…twice. To steady his nerves, he looked up at the sky for some solace. One by one, the stars were starting to come out of their hiding places. To the east, the light of the rising full moon lit up the backside of the ridge. Jason took a deep breath of crisp Rocky Mountain air, as a shooting star streaked across the night sky. It was a sign. The spirit was stirring. He was ready.

When they reached the barn, Ula asked Jessica and Jason to wait outside, so she could make a brief introduction. Within a few moments, she ushered them in to one of the most unforgettable weekends of their lives. When Jason stepped across the threshold, two things happened simultaneously. First, he was shocked to see everyone stand up, like he was a judge entering a courtroom. Second, he slipped into an unbelievably heightened state of awareness. This was a new experience. Later, he tried to put words on it, but whatever he was experiencing was far beyond the limitations of his vocabulary.

Jason scanned the gathering of about 50, looking for famous people and dignitaries. No luck there. However, he noticed almost every ethnicity was represented. Plus, there were light orbs of disembodied consciousness, floating around like soap bubbles. There were even a few members who clearly were not human. They were humanoid in shape but enveloped in wispy colorful auras. They also seemed to possess an exceptionally high level of intelligence.

"Okay, then," Jason said to himself, "This won't be normal. What was I expecting anyway?"

The only person Jason recognized was his old friend, seated in the third row back. It was Anandaji, beaming from ear to ear. As soon as Jason laid eyes on him, he bowed, as tears of joy welled up. He was humbled beyond belief and thought, "If this group is filled with peers of Anandaji, then this is a masterful audience, indeed. How on God's green Earth did I ever end up here?"

As honored as Jason was to share company with this incredible consortium, he came with his own agenda and got straight to the point. He was about to lay his two new ideas on the Council. Without hesitation, he stepped up to the podium and said, "Thank you so much for inviting me here this weekend. I'm truly honored. I'm sure Ula has briefed you on the Oracle and I'm very excited to share it with you. However, I have two conditions. First, I'd like to lead you through a meditation with the Oracle." Everyone nodded in eager anticipation at that idea. "And second," Jason continued, "when I leave here this weekend, the Oracle will no longer belong to me. I'm donating it to the Council. Furthermore, I'm asking you to decide if that is acceptable right now, before we meditate. I'd like to have that issue settled before the weekend begins. I'll be in my room, waiting for your answer." That sent a buzzing murmur through the room.

Jason graciously dismissed himself and stepped outside. Jessica and Ula remained in the barn. For a few moments, he felt like the loneliest man on the planet. He felt like he had turned his back on his own people, dumping an enormous responsibility on Ula. However, things being as they were, he needed to keep his composure. So, stiffening his upper lip, he said to himself, "So be it. I can't carry it any farther. I've done all I can do." Then he marched off to his room.

It only took about 20 minutes for Ula to fetch Jason. She innocently poked her head inside his door and said with sparkling eyes, "The Council has joyfully accepted your conditions. Honestly Jason, most of us have anticipated this for quite some time. We're deeply grateful. You been a marvelous torch bearer."

"Well, that's a load off," Jason thought, as he skipped back to the barn. "Guess the joke's on me. Joke or no joke, I'm glad to get rid of it. Now, the Oracle is free. I suppose I am too."

Triangle Seven
Jason blushed when he stepped back into the barn and nervously babbled a few incoherent words. Seeing his obvious anxiety, Ula stepped in and said, "Jason, I believe you mentioned earlier, you'd like to lead us in meditation. It would be a beautiful way to kick off the meeting."

Jason nodded, smiled, and suddenly felt back in his element. Now it was time to launch his other idea. He went straight to work, setting up the Oracle amidst the subdued oooohs and aaaahs of the audience. They'd all heard stories but now they were getting to see it in person. There's nothing like live entertainment.

Immediately, the Oracle started to glow and sparkle, like never before. It sprang to life and energetically acknowledged everyone in the room, by casting loving energy into each person's heart. It reminded Jason of his childhood, when his lost dog was joyfully reunited with his family. The Oracle had finally found its home. Everyone felt accepted and connected. It was beautiful.

Jason kept his focus and moved directly into the meditation. His idea was very simple. He was going to use his new spiritual talent from the Hawaiian Goddess and apply it to the Council. By focusing the group's will, he hoped to manifest the next triangle.

He used his soothing voice in a relaxing cadence to guide the group into a deep meditative state. As soon as he felt right, Jason asked the group to focus its attention on the Oracle and create triangle number seven.

Within seconds, the Oracle brightened, exuding an energy of purpose and confidence. Slowly, a new triangular panel emerged from thin air and gently set itself into place. Then, the Oracle rose off its stand and rotated in mid-air. With each rotation, it cast off small symbols of golden light, geometric shapes and glyphs of all kinds. Each flying symbol found a member of the Council and entered their heart, releasing a Divine energy of the highest caliber. Jason could only guess the encrypted messages they might contain.

When the meditation finished, the meeting silently adjourned. Everyone needed time to integrate their experiences, accentuated by the backdrop of Montana wilderness.

Later, the Council acknowledged, information emitted by the Oracle was far beyond human understanding. It was also recognized as essential, during this pivotal point in history. Things like fear, greed and hate simply had to go. They were ancestral weights, anchored into the fabric of human DNA. All the conscious effort and intention in the world couldn't eliminate them. There had to be Divine intervention and the Oracle embodied that help. Plus, it was in a form humans could easily assimilate. The Oracle was what they'd been waiting for. Everyone at the meeting knew it. It represented a major shift, destined to have a dramatic impact on the future of humanity.

Montana Meeting
The remainder of the meeting was like no other Jason or Jessica had ever been to. It wasn't an elite think tank with agendas, creating a plan of action to implement into the world. Not even close. In fact, it was nearly the opposite. Most everyone dropped their analytical minds at the door. That set the stage for a collective experience of surrendering to Divine will.

The rest of the weekend was spent between silent meditations with the Oracle and changelings given by the wispy humanoids. Both types of events were extremely powerful. However, Jason found the channeling sessions to be a bit of a stretch. Messages were transmitted in Vulcan, Klingon or some other extraterrestrial language he didn't understand. However, the energy that came though expanded their electrical circuits, enabling reception of higher Divine frequencies. For most Council members, the process was physically uncomfortable. For a few others, it was flat-out painful. Everyone was being rewired. It was a spiritual boot camp and it wasn't always fun.

Between meditations and changelings, there was plenty of free time to socialize or assimilate the experiences in private. Jason always opted to socialize. He figured it was a once a lifetime opportunity to schmooze with an eclectic band of spiritual high rollers.

Jason referred to the Council members as second tier operators. There were no CEOs, no presidents, no recognized leaders. However, there were plenty of advisors, vice presidents and second-in-commands. Most members intentionally flew just under the radar. There were representatives from Apple, Google, the Vatican, the IMF, the United Nations, several global humanitarian organizations, the Dali Lama's council, Findhorn, Oneness University, Auroville, a couple of doctors, several well respected researchers, a successful movie producer, artists, writers, musicians, and an assistant to the famous Brazilian healer, John of God. Ula and Hakeem sprinkled in a little international royalty for flavor.

By the end of the weekend, the overall perception within the Council had changed. With the arrival of the Oracle, visibility, activity, and responsibility were going to dramatically increase. Their mission was coming to a head and time was of the essence. They decided to continue on with what Jason had already begun, by keeping the show on the road. The only difference would be the venues. It was time to go global. By the end of the weekend, Ula already had booked the Oracle's first international showing at the Vatican's Sistine Chapel, between Christmas and New Year.

When Ula and Hakeem left on Sunday evening, they informed Jason and Jessica they were now honorary Council members and their participation was welcome, in any capacity. She reiterated by saying, "Jason, your role with the Oracle isn't finished yet. You still have an important role to play."

However, Jason wasn't so sure. He was grateful to be free of the Oracle and the responsibility it carried. He was also grateful for the weekend's meditations and his new friends. But more than all that, he was grateful to see Anandaji one more time. He wasn't sure they would ever meet again. However, Anandaji parted with a shot of reassurance by saying, "We're not done yet my friend. And my suspicion is we may never be."

The following morning, everyone was gone except Jason and Jessica. After breakfast, they too, began their long treks back. Jason was thinking about Anandaji when Jessica pulled out onto the highway. However, Jessica wanted Jason all to herself. So she hung an unexpected left to take the lover's loop, through the marvels of Yellowstone National Park.

The Oracle Goes Global
Within two years, the Oracle was a household name. By the time of the Vatican showing, Ula had scheduled a 30-month tour, to 50 different locations worldwide. She started out in Unity Council strongholds, like Oneness University and Findhorn. But by the end, the Oracle had circled the globe, leaving in its wake thousands of healings and spiritual awakenings. It even managed to slip through some intense cultural barriers. Jason was particularly awed by the diverse support from religions of nations at the Wailing Wall in Jerusalem.

However, the Oracle didn't work everywhere. In fact, in some cases it produced the exact opposite effect. The Council really went out on a limb when it tried to show the Oracle in a war-torn middle eastern county. A cease fire had been negotiated and it seemed like the perfect opportunity to establish peace. However, on the eve of the Oracle's arrival, tensions escalated. Fighting erupted into the most intense phase of the six-year war. The arrival of the Oracle only brought unresolved hatred up to the surface.

The Council estimated by the end of the tour, with enormous assistance from the Internet, nearly one billion people had been exposed to the Oracle. It was synergy in action. One small group of people were producing a massive result, larger than the sum of its individual pieces. However, their mission wasn't complete. One triangle was still needed to form it into a diamond-shaped octahedron. Furthermore, the Council knew the last triangle would come through the hands of children. Indigo Children.

Indigo Children
Indigo Children were kids believed to possess special spiritual gifts, serving as guides into the next stage of human evolution. Some of their gifts included telepathy, elevated empathy, and enhanced creativity. When it became known the last triangle was to come through children, the Council kept a sharp eye out for Indigos during the global tour. There weren't a lot of them, but a few popped out everywhere they went. At the end of two years, the Council carefully selected eleven children, all from different countries. They were scheduled to convene in New Zealand, with the hope of creating the eighth golden triangle.

The Last Triangle(s)
Ula and Hakeem invited Jason and Jessica to join them on New Zealand's south island, at Lake Wakatipu, to meet the Indigo Children. Because they threw in paid airfare as an enticement, Jason jumped all over it like white on rice.

Ula and a few members of the Unity Council arranged a weeklong event for the children and their parents. It was mostly geared toward fun with special "creativity sessions," aimed at making a new triangle. It was also a vacation for Council members, which was desperately needed, after two years of spanning the globe.

At the beginning of the first creativity session, Ula gave a presentation on the Oracle's history: the shift in global consciousness, spiritual awakening, and the important task of creating a new triangle. The only problem was, she was speaking to the kids like adults. And she was losing them fast. Within a few minutes, feet were scuffling, kids were sitting on their hands, yawns were stretching faces, and the birds flying overhead captured lost and drifting attention spans. The Titanic was sinking like a brick. Jason needed to act fast. He cut in for an emergency intervention.

From Jason's casual observations, it was obvious they were a special collection of children, ranging from seven to twelve years old. To say they were intelligent would have been an insult. These kids were geniuses. They were bilingual or multilingual; several of them in four or more languages. All of them were some type of prodigy, either in science, math, computers, music, dance, singing, sports, writing or all of the above. A few were so telepathic, Jason referred to them as the Mind Readers. They were all kind, courteous, polite and well-mannered. Jason was so astonished, he thought, "Geez, I bet they even chew with their mouths closed."

But most amazing was their awareness of spirituality. They were energetically plugged in, born as awakened spiritual masters. No wonder they didn't grasp the notion of global awakening. They were already there. They could sense and move energy without thinking about it. Healing was second nature. They could manifest at will.

Jason knew these kids were superior to him in every way. How was he to captivate their brilliant attention? Suddenly, he had an idea. Then, he moved in for the kill.

"Okay, listen up you little brats."

That got their attention. They knew this guy was going to be fun.

"Here's the deal. We're going to hold you guys prisoner at this resort for the next week until you make a magic triangle. It has to be about this big (he held up his hands) and it has to be made of gold or light or something like that. You can make it on your own or you can make it with your friends. But, whoever makes one gets an extra scoop of ice cream for dessert."

"That's the plan. Have at it."

Jason no more than finished his last sentence, when every kid jumped up and bolted out the door. The race was on.

Instinctively, each one of them ran down to the beach and started digging in the sand. Apparently, they knew something Jason didn't because they spent the rest of the day down there. By dinner, they had not one, but eleven new golden triangles. Each one was as unique as its creator. Even better, they were all the correct size and shape. If that wasn't enough, each triangle was made from some type of semi-solid light. Jason couldn't believe it. He asked one of the kids how he did it. The kid gawked at Jason, like he asked the stupidest question in the world and replied, "I used my imagination-mind, dumbo."

Jason bit his tongue, then sheepishly asked, "Gee, do you think you could teach me?"

The kid paused for a moment, as if he were surveying Jason's aura and replied, "Probably not."

So much for Jason's ego. At least he got an extra scoop of ice cream along with all the children, only because he was the one dishing out the ice cream.

By the end of the week, Jason realized they had a problem. Which triangle was the right one for the Oracle? When he asked the group of kids, Camila, a wonderful dark-haired and dark-eyed nine-year-old girl from Argentina, stood up and said, "They're all the right one. We just have to put them together."

Jason wasn't sure what she was talking about. But all the other kids nodded in agreement, as if nothing could be more natural.

So, like the true dunce that he was, Jason put the question to the kids, "And how are we going to put them together?"

In unison they all yelled, "With our imagination-minds, dumbo."

"Of course!...silly me," Jason blushed. "Well...if you're ready then. Let's do it!"

The little contingency of Indigos immediately scattered. In a few minutes, they all returned with their golden triangles. Under the direction of Camila, the children stacked them up, eleven high. Then, they closed their eyes, with child-like concentration. Within a few seconds, the triangles fused into one.

Jason's jaw dropped to the floor. He couldn't believe what the little miracle makers were capable of. Automatically, his inferiority complex kicked into overdrive. Scrambling to maintain control, as the higher ranking being in the room, he said, "Wait here. I'll be right back with the ice cream."

Later that evening, Ula heard about the miraculous triangle infusion and went to find Jason. She convinced him to take the triangle with him back to the US. Jason resisted at first. However, Ula was convinced the triangle fittings were meant for him. After all, he'd been in on all of them. She'd only assisted with two. Furthermore, she didn't feel ready. She hadn't unwound from the two year tour and needed time to settle in back home. Plus, there would be numerous decisions and arrangements to be made for the next Oracle event. For Ula, the new triangle was too much pressure. It was much better off in Jason's hands.

Ula also had an ulterior motive. If Jason kept the triangle, he'd have to come to the next triangle fitting. That way she'd get to see her friend again. "Jason," she said, "you're the one who started this amazing Oracle business. It only seems right that you put the bow on top." Jason smiled and gracefully submitted. It didn't take much arm twisting for him to want to please Ula.

Camila's Gift
It was another beautiful meeting, ended with another round of tearful goodbyes. Over the course of the week, Jason grew to adore the Indigos, especially Camila. It wasn't a hard thing to do. After all, they were little bundles of unconditional love.

After breakfast on the last day, Camila timidly approached Jason, hiding something behind her back. Blushing, she thrust out her arm with a gift and said, "Jason, this is for you. Thank you for being my friend." It was a beautifully embroidered velvet case for the triangle. She'd been working on it all week. At first, she thought she was making for herself but when the eleven triangles fused into one, she realize she was making it for him.

Jason proudly accepted her gift with a big hug. "You and I are friends forever," he whispered in her ear. Then he took her to the triangle and let her slip it into its new case.

Live Internet
When Ula and Hakeem returned to their main home in Switzerland, they decided to go underground. They seriously needed rest. Plus, they had to devise a master plan for the pinnacle showing of the Oracle. That required privacy.

In the mean time, they wanted to keep the Oracle visible. So Hakeem arranged live, one-hour showings, three times a week, at an undisclosed location. It was all done on the Internet. There was no dialogue, no introduction, no promotion. It was simply silent, live viewing. The results were remarkable. By the end of the third week, one showing reported over 600 million viewers. And the numbers were growing. Hakeem concluded that could only mean one thing. People were having spiritual experiences through their phones, computers and TVs. Physical proximity wasn't necessary for the Oracle to work.

A few days after the 600 million viewing, Jason received a call. It was Ula. She and Hakeem had regained their strength and were ready to schedule the next triangle fitting. She wanted Jason's input on location. That was a no-brainer for Jason. Without giving it a moment's thought, he confidently blurted out, "Fiji."

Fiji it was. However, Ula decided to opt against holding it open to the public. Instead, it would be a quiet affair, open to Unity

Council members only. They'd simply film it live over the Internet for everyone else. Jason supported that idea whole-heartedly.

The meeting was scheduled for early June. Until then, Hakeem continued live viewings over the Internet. At the end of each showing, he added simple text, indicating the time and date of the final triangle placement. By the middle of May, viewers topped 900 million.

The Elder Returns
It had been almost three years since Montana. Jason and Jessica were excited to see their friends from the Council again. Almost everyone who attended the meeting in Montana was present in Fiji. However, there were a few fresh faces and several senior members had crossed over, now helping from the other side.

Jason was gifted with another joyous reunion with Anandaji. However, even more surprising and delightful, was the unexpected arrival of Camila. As soon as she saw Jason, she sprinted across the lawn and jumped into his arms, exchanging "the biggest bear hug in the world." Camila's presence made it obvious. The time to complete the Oracle had come.

The triangle fitting was scheduled for early Saturday afternoon. On the evening before, the Council congregated for a brief centering meditation. Ula began by setting up the Oracle, with the idea of leaving it on display for the entire weekend. As she placed the Oracle on its stand, one of the largest full moons in recorded history emerged from the eastern horizon, beginning its magnificent voyage across the expansive South Pacific sky. Magic was most certainly in the air.

The next day was beautiful. There wasn't a cloud to be seen. Yet, the campus on which they were located was eerily quiet. The previous evening, everyone had voted to remain in silence until the final fitting was completed. The nervous anticipation the silence created hovered noticeably in the air. You could have rung it like a bell.

The doors to the community longhouse, where the event was held, were wide open. They perfectly framed the surf, breaking over a distant reef, like a priceless piece of living artwork. Fresh tropical bouquets were cut and placed on a simple alter, filling the room with a magnificent fragrance. The triangle lay waiting between the flowers. The Oracle was placed front and center, immediately in front of the open doors and the alter. The stage was set; cameras were ready to roll.

Everyone in the Council was situated fifteen minutes before show time. It was up to each individual to prepare themselves as they saw fit. Jason and Jessica were seated up front and off to one side, next to Ula and Hakeem. The rest of the council was seated in front of the small stage. Jason took one look around the room. Based the on the expressions of faces, it seemed everyone was pretty nervous.

The plan was simple. Five minutes after the cameras starting filming, Jason was to walk up on stage and place the triangle in the Oracle. Nothing to it.

He tried to breathe deeply and remain calm but it was useless. So he just sat there and nervously fiddled around.

3...2...1...Roll 'em. It was show time.

Five minutes later, Jason received his hand signal from the cameraman. Slowly, he pulled himself to his feet and stoically walked up on stage. As he approached the alter, he saw Camila sitting next to her parents in the front row. "No time like the present to improvise," he thought. So with his index finger, he motioned to Camila to join him on stage. She froze like a deer in the headlights and looked to her Mom for protection. She was no help. She coaxed her to stand up and go on stage.

Jason gently grabbed Camila by the hand and walked her over to the altar. Without saying a word, he tilted his head at the triangle. Camila immediately understood and gingerly picked it up. Jason then lifted her from the waist like a ballerina and gracefully marched her over to the Oracle. From there, the Oracle gracefully took it off her hands.

It was a perfect fit. Slowly, the diamond-shaped Oracle lifted off its stand and began to rotate, suspended in mid-air. Just like in Montana, it cast glyphs of golden light out into the audience. Everyone was mesmerized.

After several minutes, an image of similar golden light appeared next to the Oracle. It was the Inuit Elder from Chevron Mountain. This time, he didn't materialize physically but simply hovered, visible from the chest up, illuminated. Blinking periodically, he didn't say a word but just stared into space, as if he were aligned with a presence far beyond the reach of mere mortals.

After what seemed like a timeless eternity, he began to speak in Inuit. Jason had no idea how it worked, but again, he understood every word he said. Slowly, deliberately and with utter conviction, he began. "Welcome my brothers and sisters…Today marks the day of great transition…It is a day of destiny, built on the shoulders of countless generations…It has been created from infinite choices, choices made by you and all of your ancestors."

Jason glanced around to check the vibe in the room. Energy was swirling and swelling like a funnel cloud made of electricity.

The Elder continued, "It is also a day of separation, a time for parting and splitting. It is time to divide left from right, positive from negative, light from dark."

Jason's mouth gaped open and his heart seized. He couldn't believe what he was hearing. His mind went nuts. "This was supposed to be a movement toward unity. An era of wholeness and oneness. He'd spent his entire adult life committed and dedicated toward that goal. And now the Elder was pulling the rug? You mean, all along it had been a game of Spy vs. Spy, Good vs. Evil, Jesus against Lucifer?"

He felt like he'd been duped, a sucker in the greatest con game of all time—a supporting actor in a bad sci-fi movie. His entire perception of the Universe was instantly shattered before his very eyes. What was infinitely worse, was that he was losing it in front of people he held most dear.

Lucky for Jason, he was seated between Jessica and Ula. Ula noticed Jason's distress and quickly leaned over, whispering in his ear, "It's okay…it's okay. We'll talk when it's over. Everything will be all right." Then she gave Jessica a glance saying, "Quick, give him a hug." She did. Jason immediately starting bawling like a little baby.

Unwavering, the Elder continued, "The people of our Earth Mother are responding to the forces of Nature…It is the path of the river, the ocean and the sky…The change taking place is undeniable as the twinkling stars above…There is no right…There is no wrong…There only is what is…It is for you to choose…And the time is now…Choose the Light and be not afraid…Your ancestors are with you."

With the utterance of his final words, the Elder condensed into a brilliant ball of golden light and drifted into the center of the spinning Oracle. Immediately, the ball transformed and illuminated into incandescent platinum light. Then it started to expand. All the while, the Oracle continued to spin, casting glyphs of gold into the audience.

With each surge of expansion, the ball became lighter and more translucent. When it reached about four feet in diameter, it was barely visible. The Oracle remained centered inside, spinning, suspended. It was a moment for the ages, lucidly burned into the banks of Jason's memory forever.

After what seemed like an instant and an eternity combined, the ball burst like a soap bubble. Everyone instinctively cringed, expecting a resonating wave of shock. However, a deeply embedded layer of denseness began to lift off and dissolve from each person in the room.

The Oracle continued spinning, faster and faster, dissolving the unseen layer of weight that had crippled humanity since the beginning of time. It contained primordial fear, violence of all kinds, hatred, greed, lust—all the undeveloped reptilian emotions, held hostage by the need to control and survive.

As the tremendous burden released, Jason felt an internal split developing in his soul. It seemed every choice he'd ever made suddenly straddled the fence. Everything was hanging in the balance. He recognized it was the critical moment of a defining decision, a time to align with his values, a time of conviction, a time to choose.

Without hesitation, he chose the Light.

Meanwhile, The Oracle continued, spinning itself into an absolute frenzy, until the layer of denseness was lifted off completely. Then, as it hit fever pitch, the Oracle exploded into a million shards of brilliant golden light, landing in the hearts and minds of all who watched.

And just like that, the Oracle was gone. Jason burst into the laughter of a major emotional release, while the rest of the Council recoiled, stunned into silence. No one moved until the filming stopped, well over an hour later. In the end, Ula stood up and made an awkward concluding statement. "I think that's enough for one day. Let's meet back here tomorrow, after breakfast."

That was it. What took over twenty years of discernment, action and waiting was over in a matter of minutes. There was nothing left to do but silently disperse. No one spoke a word until after breakfast the next morning.

Polarity and Separation

The meeting the next morning was not the usual meditation/channeling session. Far from it. It was a debriefing and discussion, pure and simple. Everyone was interested in comparing notes, trying to piece together what the heck had happened the day before.

The consensus was unanimous. It was a discharge of negative, genetically-inherited memory and the primordial denseness that went with it. Even the extraterrestrials felt the release. Furthermore, a number of the Council members had already been in contact with friends and family who watched the transmission over the Internet. Reports were coming in from all over the world of similar experiences. Remarkably, it was estimated that close to 1.3 billion people viewed the event.

It was also clear, everyone felt some type of internal split, combined with a need to make a defining decision. For many, if felt like an ultimatum—choose Light or otherwise. Also, it was apparent the shift wasn't limited to an internal personal experience. Humanity itself was splitting apart.

Jason learned, in the months leading up to the Fiji showing, a number of seers within the Council had received critical information from higher realms. Independent sources from opposite ends of the Earth concurred on the content. Humanity, as well as the Earth itself, was dividing into two separate and unconnected parallel universes.

According to the seers, the enormous energy gap, created by millenniums of opposing mentalities, was at a breaking point. The chasm between violence and hatred in relation to healing and awakening had simply grown too wide. The energetic divergence was unstoppable; separation was inevitable. It wasn't so much Divine will as it was a submission to the laws of quantum physics. Like attracts like. Both worlds were eventually heading to the same place. However, they were temporarily traveling in opposite directions.

Those in the Council who weren't seers, like Jason, pounded the visionaries with numerous questions. They wanted to know about the future and the result of the split.

They seers gladly shared their insights. What follows is the gist of their visions:

Both worlds will continue to physically exist, only in different energetic dimensions. However, for the most part, the separation will go undetected on the physical plane. There will be a few signs, such as changing climate, violent storms, and a likely magnetic reversal of the poles. Furthermore, outcomes will be strongly influenced by how people in each dimension respond. Earthly disruptions can be an opportunity for growth, awakening and healing or they can be omens of doom and destruction. Choice and perception will always be the driving forces behind destiny.

During the split, individuals will align with their chosen world, one awakened and one not. For a brief period, a minority of souls will be caught between the two worlds. They will remain there, quite uncomfortable, until they decide where they want to belong.

There will be a few evolved individuals who will maintain contact between the two worlds, using psychic awareness. Their job will be to assist in the separation, until it is complete. After that, the two worlds will become so foreign, they will no longer recognize each other, not even on an energetic level.

Most of the shift into a higher state will happen in the subconscious mind, readily recognized by people who are awakened. That level of awareness will align with higher vibrations, creating miracles on a global level that seem impossible to us today. Technologies will continue to evolve but will serve as tools, instead of a means to steal and distract our attention. People will be the masters of their technology, not visa-versa. In addition, families will no longer be fragmented, cooperation and diplomacy will be the norm, economies will balance, the Earth will heal, and populations will gravitate to a healthy and sustainable level.

Furthermore, the broken systems created by humanity will start to mend; politics will govern the needs of the people, the legal system will uphold justice, the health care system will serve the sick, education will nurture creativity and guide all toward improving the quality of life, and the financial system will distribute wealth fairly. In short, the systems of the world will serve their intended purposes, no longer acting as structures to hoard power, position and money. That's because the underlying motivations of inherited fear and greed will be gone.

However, the transition will not be rapid. Expect at least a generation for it to phase in completely. Plus, there will be a few bumps along the way.

It's best not to place your attention on the separation, because it will happen whether you pay attention or not. Instead, focus on improving the quality of your lives. Fully embrace the act of living. Enjoy this miraculous shift in being.

Chapter 11
The New World

The Inner World

If the seers were right, Jason knew he'd be lucky to live long enough to see the results play out. However, he couldn't wait to get home and see if there were any initial effects. The first thing he noticed on the return flight was how good he felt. It was more of a pervasive relief than anything else, as if a chronic stress he'd carried his entire life was suddenly gone.

When Jason got home, he took a stroll down to the bay. Before walking half a block, he stopped and chatted with a neighbor who was working in his garden. The latest gossip was that the local drug dealer, who lived about a block down the street, moved away. No one knew if he had been arrested or if he had skipped town trying to avoid it. Whatever the case, everyone in the neighborhood was thrilled. "Hmm...," Jason thought. "A layer of neighborhood mayhem has certainly vanished. If that's what the shift in consciousness is about, I'm all in."

Over the course of the next week, Jason paid careful attention to his inner workings. The most notable realizations were about the first emotions he felt when he woke up. For as long as he could remember, the first sensation he had each day was fear. Usually, the fear was seasoned with a touch of depression. It lived right between his heart and his stomach. On most days, after a morning meditation and a hot shower, the fear evaporated. However, it was a sad realization to admit his entire life was framed by such feelings.

Since Fiji, those feelings were gone. Furthermore, their absence was as subtle as it was profound. What Jason felt now was mild contentment, tinged with a touch of happiness. On top of that, was a sense of reassurance that no matter what happened, everything would be okay. Whatever had happened in Fiji, had shifted his entire perception of reality. Contentment and happiness replaced fear and depression. It wasn't obvious but it was utterly transforming.

Over the next few months, Jason didn't feel compelled to meditate. The states of mind he tried to achieve with meditation were now permanent parts of his life. He often felt peaceful and energized, with periodic flashes of joy. Furthermore, when he did meditate, mystical experiences and amazing new worlds awaited. The gifts from the Hawaiian Goddess were always available and new ones emerged as needed. He'd never felt so integrated, alive and aligned with his life's purpose.

The Outer World
By the end of the year, Jessica and Jason had gotten to know most of their neighbors. A genuine sense of community was starting to develop. Thinking back over the course of his adult life, Jason realized, that no matter where he lived, he had never connected with his neighbors. He'd always assumed that being an American meant living in isolation. The shift occurring on his street, seemed like a major miracle indeed.

As the holiday season approached, Jason also noted conversations among neighbors, friends and colleagues. They were rarely negative; no one was dreading family gatherings. Jason thought, "Is the shift in consciousness really running that deep? Is it actually healing relationships within families? A transformation of that magnitude will reconstruct the psyche of humanity. If that doesn't change the world, nothing will."

*

The Big Picture
It had been five years since Fiji and the disappearance of the Oracle. In spiritual circles it was now being referred to as the beginning of the "Golden Age." Jason and Jessica were now married, living their destined paths in a new city. They'd also been to a few

Unity Council meetings that seemed more like wonderful reunions than visionary meetings of global transformation.

However, the meetings were significant because they noted changes happening on the planet. First on most people's radar was the stabilization of global financial markets. Stock markets that had fluctuated in a torrent of chaos had seen five years of relatively stable growth. Next, the military powers of the West had negotiated lasting peace settlements with insurgency factions, while other hotspots on the globe seemed to be cooling. Social unrest and violence were on a significant decline. Words like superpower, rogue state and terrorism were rarely mentioned in the media. Furthermore, the media itself seemed to be shifting focus, not nearly as obsessed with violence. It just wasn't selling. What now captured the public's interest was a more balanced account of events. If that wasn't enough, several large environmental coalitions were making documented progress on cleaning water supplies, preventing pollution of the oceans, and reversing the trends in global warming. Furthermore, older generations were dropping like flies and the younger populace was showing a moderate decline in birth rates. For the first time in the history of the planet, human population was slowly decreasing. From a broad perspective, the global outlook was optimistic, something it hadn't been in generations.

As nice as all that was, Jason wasn't too concerned about global affairs. What mattered to him was that he and Jessica were genuinely happy, something neither of them had been able to sustain before. Plus, they were excited and actively involved in all aspects of their lives. Jason thought if others were experiencing as much improvement in life as he was, then the Oracle was a smashing success.

The Next Generation
Fast forward—sometime later. It was a beautiful spring day. Jason and Jessica were out on a stroll. When they arrived at a nearby park, they grabbed a bench to enjoy the sunshine of a nearly perfect day.

Across the way were about 10 children making a bunch of racket at what looked like a birthday party. Jason sat and casually observed their celebratory shenanigans. After a few moments, he realized they were all pre-schoolers, born after the end of the Oracle. He wondered if they were highly evolved old souls. From his vantage point, they didn't seem like anything special, just normal kids.

As soon as that notion wafted through, a gust of wind kicked up and blew a beach ball from the party, straight at Jason. One of the party goers took chase in hot pursuit. However, she couldn't catch up with it before it rolled to a stop at his feet.

Jason, being the imp he always was, held onto the ball, waiting to toy with the approaching tot. He was taken by how much she reminded him of Camila. As she ran up and came to a halt, she gave Jason an expression that said, "Please Mister, give my ball back."

Jason replied, "I'll give it back, if you tell me a secret."

She returned a look of playful disgust and said, "Oh…all right…" Then she paused and thought for a moment, like she was posing a question to herself. After receiving her answer, she replied, "We all are."

Jason, playing along with her little game, replied, "Oh…you are, are you? And what is it you all are?"

"Indigo Children," she beamed. Then she snatched the ball, squealed with delight, and bolted back to the party.

Jason stared on in amused disbelief as she skipped across the grass. For the second time in his life, he was able to see her soft golden aura. In quiet admiration, he quietly laughed to himself, feeling very glad to be a part of this world.

Other books by Joseph Drumheller

The Subconscious the Divine and Me
A spiritual guide for the day to day pilgrim

An easy-to-read, yet profound, introduction into the mystical worlds of subconscious healing and spirituality. Through six lessons, Joseph Drumheller leads us from pain we feel to the ability to take action and create better lives.

1. Pain Leads to Suffering
2. Suffering Leads to Awareness
3. Awareness Leads to Healing
4. Healing Leads to Awakening
5. Awakening Leads to Development
6. Development Leads to Action

To stay in touch, sign up on my mailing list and get the latest on books, events and all sorts of fun:

www.josephdrumheller.com

Review it!

If you loved my book, I'd love to read your review. Please go to amazon.com, type in my name at the top, click on the book, and let the world know what you think!

Made in the USA
San Bernardino, CA
13 June 2015